# THE HEALTHY EDGE
# COOKBOOK
## YOUR EASY & DELICIOUS GUIDE TO LIVE BY

THE
HEALTHYEDGE ™
LIVE THE ABUNDANT LIFE

**THE**
**HEALTHYEDGE** ™
*LIVE THE ABUNDANT LIFE*

To purchase additional copies or bulk order of *The Healthy Edge Cookbook*
please visit us at:

**TheHealthyEdgeCookbook.com**
*or*
**GetTheHealthyEdge.com**

• • • • • • • • • • • • • • • • • • • • • • • • • • • • • • • • • • • • • • •

# THE HEALTHY EDGE COOKBOOK

The information in this book is not intended to replace medical advice from a physician. The material contained in The Healthy Edge Cookbook is for general information and the purpose of educating individuals on health, nutrition, lifestyle and other related topics. For those people with food or other allergies, or who have specific food require-ments, all recipes should be reviewed thoroughly to determine whether they contain any ingredient(s) that may pose a problem for you. Before beginning this or any nutritional, fitness, or exercise program, consult your physician or other qualified health care provider to be sure it is appropriate for you.

The average results of an individual who completed The Healthy Edge program, as described, released 9.16 pounds and 2.3 total inches in their waist and hips during the six week program.

Printed in The United States of America

Design & Layout by: Innovative Graphics, Inc. • Kalispell, Montana • igprodesign.com

Printed by: Lesher Printers, Inc. • Fremont, Ohio • lesherprinters.com

This book is dedicated to our mother

# Arlene Brenamen

Her life and death inspired it's creation.

● ● ● ● ●

We thank God everyday
for each moment we had with her
on this earth.

# ACKNOWLEDGEMENTS

To our husbands, Brian and Brandon, who love and support us on a daily basis. You know our hearts and faithfully follow us in our purpose. We love you. To precious Arleena, who reminds us every day why we do what we do. Special thanks to Brian for his talents that were crucial in the creation of this cookbook. You are irreplaceable!

Words can't describe our gratitude to Jack and Lorraine Zimmerman, who believed in us and have continued to support us in getting this vision out to the world!

To our families: Dad, Carla, Adrianne, Dean, Ryleigh and Kobe; Brandon's parents; Jan and Rick Willer and Brian's parents; Jim and Charity Thiel. Thank you for your unconditional love and support.

Our deepest appreciation and thanks to Chef Keith for creating the recipes and bringing this book to life. And to Mindy Mosser who spent countless hours on this project. Also, to Mindy's mom, Teresa Tritt, and to Bob and Terri Mosser for all their support.

Our gratitude also goes to Nate Horton and Innovative Graphics for the layout, design and organization of this book that reflects the passion and heart of The Healthy Edge. We appreciate your friendship and partnership.

We feel blessed to have so many incredible businesses and professionals supporting us! A noteworthy thanks to Joe and Garry at EnCorpus, Adam Patel at MaxImpactOnline, Nems at Three Chicks Catering, Jon and Carol Eklof for marketing and editing support, Mykal and Maryum at Kona Kai Coffee Company, Ed Griffin at Hardcastle Entertainment, Kieran and Sherri Murry at Kieran's List, Roger King at RKM productions, Renee at Able Embroidery, Troy at Post Net, Klemmer & Associates, Jacqueline DeFriece at Highlander Photography, Ralph's Joy of Living, Rheim's Farmer's Market, and TK, Adam and Doug from BAS Broadcsting Ohio. An heart felt thanks to our family at Lesher Printers, Inc. in Fremont, Ohio, thank you for being a part of our lives and this project! Big hugs to our dad, Guy, for all of his hard work in printing this book! Thank you to Dr. Mark Zakowski and Dr. Mark Roberto for your inspiring words.

We can't express how humbled we are by the life transformation that occurs daily from the efforts of our Independent Facilitators around the world that have breathed life into The Healthy Edge.

While there are too many to list, our deepest thanks go to our friends and family that surround our lives in love and support. This journey has brought us all together and we are so blessed to be changing the world alongside you!

To our Healthy Edge family around the world and everyone that will take the journey in the future; we love and believe in you and look forward to continuing to support you in your Abundant Life.

Most importantly, thanks to our Lord Jesus Christ, for saving us, giving us life and blessing us with every good thing.

# TABLE OF CONTENTS

The Health Care Debate has been raging for months, with the politicians, insurance companies, drug companies—and yes, even some physicians—getting it all wrong. The nation has been spending too much on Health Care, over 2.2 trillion dollars at last count, and we are getting woefully too little in return. The US ranks near the bottom of infant mortality among industrialized nations. Pretty sad, don't you think? We are spending more money than any nation in the world, yet we are not healthier. Why is that? The medical system is mainly focused on treating disease rather than keeping people healthy and well to avoid disease altogether. Wellness is fundamentally disease prevention. Oh, and by the way, it would be terribly cost effective for the country, too. But don't depend on the politicians to get it right. There is too much money changing hands in the system for change to occur.

The only one truly responsible for your health is YOU. As an MD, I have been advocating for better health care – by you, the individual, the patient, the pregnant mother, your friends, your relatives, by everyone. You need to take responsibility for your own health. That means being PROACTIVE in taking care of and educating yourself. Asking the right questions! You can influence your health, your wellness, and, indeed, the health care you receive from the medical system. Armed with the knowledge, respect for your own abilities, and asking the right questions, you can receive the health and care you deserve.

The first step to wellness and good health is eating well. Your body can only use the ingredients you eat to grow, function, and repair itself. Eating well, by which I mean consuming wholesome foods free of unneeded chemicals, will help to allow your body to function properly. Drinking lots of clean, pure water is also essential. Most people are partly dehydrated, making it harder for their bodies to function properly by inhibiting their ability to eliminate toxins and waste. The nutritional content of food has declined over the last 50 years, as well. You need to eat better, more wisely, and preferably organic foods.

In addition to eating wholesome foods, you need to eat intelligently. Your body is influenced by the quantity and timing of what you eat. During pregnancy, eating poorly can result in diabetes of pregnancy, with larger than normal babies, increased chance of Cesarean delivery and neonatal breathing difficulties. Indeed, maintaining a normal blood sugar is essential for long-term health, for everyone. The stages for diabetes and heart disease are set early… by what you are eating now, as well as during your 20s, 30s, and 40s. Syndrome X, now called Metabolic Syndrome, is the precursor of becoming diabetic and having heart disease. Your body develops insulin resistance, and your insulin levels increase; then, later, your blood sugar elevates and you are diabetic. Avoiding sugars and simple starches is just a start. An elevated blood sugar leads to glycation, where a sugar molecule attaches to proteins, affecting function and biologic aging and neurodegenerative diseases like Alzheimer's, and destructive reactive oxygen species (free radicals). This is the FIRST step toward not only diabetes, but also heart disease, organ dysfunction, protein and enzyme dysfunction, premature aging, and stiffening of tissues by cross-linking of these new compounds. Yet, it remains avoidable. The choice is YOURS.

*The Healthy Edge* is a wonderful start in your journey to achieve good health through prevention and wellness, by avoiding the long term health effects of the SAD—the Standard American Diet, which is rich in fats and sugars, and eating too much of it. The authors have created an easy-to-follow, great-tasting menu that will lead you to feel better, lose weight, be fit, and become healthier. They have created a wonderful and effective program that will help you to eat better and be healthy, with great tools and support for you. Amber Thiel and April Willer really bring you the outstanding information that is easy to consume… both literally and figuratively! Healthy eating, good food, easy to do—exactly what the doctor ordered!

**Dr. Mark Zakowski, MD**

*Author—The Safe Baby System*
*SafeBabySystem.com*

In over twenty-five years of clinical practice, I have recommended diets and programs for weight loss and disease-modification, and even practiced them for myself, and I have never seen as comprehensive a lifestyle and health management program as *The Healthy Edge*.

The reality is that we are undernourished and overfed. We are overwhelmed by false claims, by artificial products, by diet plans that over-promise, and by programs that single out a nutritional truth but go sideways with unproven recommendations, or worse, harmful ones. Food is much, much more than calories in the form of protein, carbohydrate and fat.

In shifting from this old paradigm, science is proving that the key to our health is taking a proactive approach through our lifestyle choices. Certain natural foods and food based compounds called phytonutrients have the power to promote healing in our body. Scientists studying nutrigenomics look at how food-based compounds have the ability to 'up-regulate' (turn on) disease-preventing genes or 'down-regulate' (turn off) disease promoting genes. Omega-3 fatty acids in fish are anti-inflammatory and lower triglycerides levels. Certain berries have the ability to make our arteries more compliant and less 'sticky', therefore less likely to develop atherosclerotic plaque build-up. Immunology and Nutritional Science show us how certain foods can bring a balance to our immune function and how low glycemic diets affect insulin and the regulation of weight and appetite, mood and behavior.

Without accountability and support, some of you may end up getting frustrated or falling 'off the wagon'. We all have mental 'tapes' and beliefs that not only do not support us, but also trigger failure mechanisms! Anyone ever failed at a diet? Many develop these beliefs innocently (ie: "I'm not good enough") due to the emotional immaturity of simply being a child when the lesson was internalized. The problems arise in our health, relationships and ego when we continue to believe it throughout our adulthood! *The Healthy Edge* combines the people, tools and mechanisms for us to be honest, authentic, committed and loving toward ourselves, and to discard non-serving belief systems. This is the key to life-long results.

*The Healthy Edge* is based on natural physiologic principles of health and nutrition, supported by scientific research, integrated into a package with broad application, teaching and truth. I challenge you to immerse yourself in what *The Healthy Edge* offers you- it will honor, nourish, and support your body and mind. Eat it, Drink it, Live it and FEEL IT!

**Dr. Mark S. Roberto, MD**

## THROUGH TRAGEDY THE HEALTHY EDGE IS BORN...

In our teens, our lives were turned upside down when our mom was diagnosed with breast cancer. For the next eight years, we watched as our mother battled an enemy that was relentless. After surgeries, radiation and several bouts of chemotherapy, there wasn't much left of the vibrant woman we had known in our childhood. The therapies themselves were slowly draining the life out of her.

Our mom led what we thought was a healthy lifestyle and was one of 9 children all of whom are healthy and living today. How could she be the one to get cancer? Late in her journey, Mom and Dad decided to put a stop to all "conventional" medicine. She turned solely to faith and nutrition. She put foods in her body that would promote healing and well-being and spent lots of quality time with those she loved.

Although the cancer was everywhere, she felt better in those last months of her life than she had throughout most of the disease. It was evident that there was power in putting in good food and supporting a mindset that nurtured healing. Our

**Amber, Mom, Adrianne, April**

mom's life was a testimony that our health is priceless, and love and faith can endure all things. There was no amount of money to restore her health although there wasn't a price we weren't willing to pay.

At the age of 45, Arlene Brenamen left this world to be with God. Her death was not the end of the story, it was only the beginning. We set out on a journey of physical and emotional health that led to the vision of *The Healthy Edge*. This book is a piece of that vision to be shared with the world.

## WHAT DO YOU BELIEVE ABOUT HEALTHY?

Have you been fed the belief that something *Healthy* can't taste good? Or that *Healthy* is hard? How about that *Healthy* is expensive? Do you listen to the media for your beliefs about *Healthy*? Are the messages that low-fat, low-carbs, artificial sweeteners, microwaveable "health" meals, fruit juices, cereals and even fast food are *Healthy* dictating your food choices?

What if your beliefs are what is holding you and your family back from health and weight release? This cookbook was created to prove that healthy eating can be simple and taste oh, so good. Our hope for you is that by experiencing the taste of healthy, you will build belief that you and your family can live the abundant life offered through *The Healthy Edge*.

8

# WHAT BELIEFS ARE HOLDING YOU BACK?

### Belief #1: *IF I AM THIN, I WILL BE HEALTHY*

Although I (Amber) was thin and athletic, I was not healthy. I experienced restless nights of sleep, suffered from depression, battled with colds 2-3 times a year and had horrible bouts of acne. What good was it to have a thin body if my insides were clearly not healthy? How many people are caught up in the belief that people who are thin feel great and are healthy? Many thin people mask their issues with their appearance, while someone carrying extra weight is stereotypically deemed as unhealthy. This is an unfair assumption and can hold thin people back from truly looking at their health. The only solution to long term weight release AND health is a healthy lifestyle.

### Belief #2: *I HAVE NO WILLPOWER*

Many people experience incredible carbohydrate cravings for bread, pasta, chips and sweets that make it feel impossible to eat healthily and lose weight. Mood swings, depression, lack of energy, trouble focusing and weight gain around the middle are common complaints. These symptoms can be directly correlated to something called Insulin Resistance and is due to consumption of highly processed foods leading to subsequent sugar spikes and dips. It's like living life on a roller coaster.

One of the most powerful gifts of *The Healthy Edge* is learning why it may not be your fault that you feel like you have no willpower. The FREE 14 day test drive of *The Healthy Edge* program will explain the concept of Insulin Resistance, how to overcome it and how you may not even be the one choosing what you eat. This alone can change your life.

Take the test drive at
**GetTheHealthyEdge.com**.
It's our gift to you!

### Belief #3: *IT'S TOO HARD*

Healthy is only hard if you make it hard. I (April) know this from personal experience. If I told you that you could never eat foods containing gluten (wheat) or dairy in order to be healthy what would you say? Most of you would shut this book or quickly go on to the next paragraph. My daughter, Arleena, and I, within the last few years, both were diagnosed with Celiac Disease. To top it off, Arleena is also allergic to Casein (the protein in milk). For my whole life, every time I put gluten into my mouth I was destroying my body. The prices I have paid for not knowing that has cost me dearly. Now that I have this knowledge, Arleena and I live a gluten and dairy-free life with ease.

What prices are you paying in your health that you may not be aware of? What knowledge do you need to uncover to take the next step in your health journey? Healthy isn't hard. It's a choice.

### THE WINNING BELIEF: *HEALTHY IS A CHOICE*

*The Healthy Edge* is all about personal choices. The choices are not right or wrong, they are yours and you own them. The belief that healthy is your choice will serve you well in life.

Making small decisions every day will make your health journey manageable and enjoyable. Our daily choices compound into our health and our health is a journey, not a destination. The best part of *The Healthy Edge* journey is that weight release is a side effect instead of your primary focus. Diets disrupt people's lives. They affect the one person on the diet and are not sustainable. A lifestyle affects everyone around you and is a way of living. How incredible to learn the tools to be empowered in every situation! Experience this life free for 14 days at **GetTheHealthyEdge.com**.

Although I was the skinny girl growing up and an athlete in high school and college, I wouldn't have labeled myself as healthy. I struggled with depression, acne, eating disorders, insomnia and daily fatigue through my teens and into my twenties. I hated the way I looked and what I was doing to myself. I counted calories, I popped diet pills, I exercised for hours, I binged, I beat myself up and the cycle continued. I would do almost anything to stay "thin and perfect."

**Amber and Brian Thiel**

Watching my mom die of breast cancer was the greatest gift and loss in my life. The gift was the reality of my mortality. I went on a journey of self growth and education that would later manifest as *The Healthy Edge*. I feel proud to say that I love myself and my body, unconditionally. The number on the scale no longer represents who I am or drives my choices. I live a life free of disease, depression, bondage and pain...and I'm thin as a side effect!

The greatest gift on my journey was finding my soul mate, Brian. Without him, the gift of *The Healthy Edge* would have never reached beyond the weekly meetings in our living room. His heart and soul is in every aspect of this program and cookbook. Brian and I travel around the world spreading this vision. We have committed our lives to redefining the health reality for future generations. We are living proof that there is a way to have it all, we can't wait to share this with you!

Amber and Brian Thiel live in Seattle, WA where they enjoy hiking, traveling, cooking, eating and spending time with friends. Amber majored in Biology and Education and graduated Summa Cum-Laude in 2000 from The University of Findlay in Ohio. In 2002, she earned a Masters of Education and began teaching and coaching. Amber was an Academic All-American volleyball player and has always had a passion for empowering and inspiring individuals to be the best they can be. She taught Biology, Anatomy and Physiology, Wellness and Human Nutrition and coached volleyball at the high school and college levels. At the age of 19, she began her own business conducting volleyball camps. At 23, she started her first health and wellness business. Amber is now a personal trainer and in 2009 was named in the top 5 personal trainers of Western Washington by King 5 News.

**Amber** was nominated for 2009 Business Examiner's Women of Influence.

As long as I can remember I have been passionate about being fit, mainly because I was always fighting the scale. I was considered "big boned" all of my life and thought it was normal to feel bloated after every meal. I remember the frustration and pain that came from fighting a battle that I didn't have the knowledge to win. On my road to health, I found supplements and a lifestyle of health and personal development that would change me forever. The final piece of the puzzle was when my daughter and I discovered we had Celiac disease and other food allergies which was the final road block that needed to be removed. It was very challenging to take all that in but I feel God only gives you what you can handle and we are thriving thanks to His perfect plan.

**The Willers**
Arleena, April, and Brandon

My amazing husband and high school sweetheart, Brandon, wasn't as quick to make the changes we now live. After a career of college football, putting him over 280 lbs at one point, and numerous injuries, his body continued to increase in pain. One day when attempting to pick up our daughter, Arleena, he literally got stuck in that position. A back surgery followed and months of recovery. Then, by the grace of God, he began living this *Healthy Edge* lifestyle with me. Today, Brandon weighs 210 lbs and feels great. He competes in marathons and finished the Chicago Olympic triathlon this year. Not bad for a guy that wasn't supposed to be able to do much after all the damage that was done to his body. We live in Fremont, OH and enjoy empowering others to live the abundant life.

We are thankful everyday for the blessings in our lives. I started my first health and wellness business over seven years ago and through that journey was able to lead and support some of the most amazing people. They grew me and challenged me in ways that I never imagined. It became very clear along my journey, that my purpose and passion is to love unconditionally and inspire people to be great! *The Healthy Edge* has allowed me to do that beyond what I imagined. I am blessed with a loving daughter who I have the privilege to teach at home and the most amazing husband I could ever ask for. Great friends, great family what else could I ask for? Thank you Jesus!

**Brandon** has released over 70 lbs. since college.

# THE HEALTHY EDGE PROGRAM

## THE HEART AND VISION OF *THE HEALTHY EDGE*

### THE HEART

Our mom, Arlene Brenamen, did not die without cause or reason... she left this vision behind for us to take to the world. She taught us that every moment that God gives us is a blessing, not a guarantee; that life is about the little things we may be missing by not truly experiencing life; that each time you leave someone you love, you kiss them and hug them and tell them you love them; that this, too, shall pass; that you can't control what life throws at you, but you can choose how you will respond to it (and the answer is always in love); that the answer to most of life's problems is to love more; that there is no time for bitterness and resentment; that the time to change is always now; and, most importantly, LIFE IS NOT ABOUT YOU but about something much bigger than you could ever comprehend.

### THE VISION

*The Healthy Edge* is about reversing the trends of obesity in children as well as adults by taking responsibility for our health and the health of our families. We believe everyone can live the abundant life they were put here on earth to live if they will only choose to take the journey. Through education, personal development and passion, *The Healthy Edge* can put you on the path to living your abundant life. Join us and start living your life on the edge with people that want to lead by example and love.

## WHAT IS *THE HEALTHY EDGE* PROGRAM?

*Well, here's what it's* **NOT!**

*IT'S NOT ANOTHER* **DIET!**

*The Healthy Edge* is a window into living life without the guilt and restraints that come from traditional weight loss programs. How would you like to release weight without calorie counting, without restrictions and eating more than you ever thought possible? Why are people always trying to lose weight just to find it again? When you put together a lifestyle that you can live with, since you are the one that needs to live it, you will be able to have long term results in your health which produces long term result in your waistline. Get off your diet and get into your head to break through all the belief systems that are keeping you from getting what you want in life.

## IT'S NOT ANOTHER "HOW TO" PROGRAM!

*If How To's Were Enough We Would All Be Skinny, Rich, and Happy,* by Brian Klemmer, is a great book if you think how to's are enough to create change in your life. *The Healthy Edge* dives deep into the belief systems that have been haunting you from childhood. Do you have any of these beliefs about health? They sound like this: I have bad genes so I will never be thin... I have to work out for hours to be healthy and fit... I am not worthy... I don't have the time...I am too old to change... I have to count calories and portion everything to lose weight... I have failed at everything else, so I am sure to fail at this. If these sound familiar, we have the tools to allow you to explode these once and for all, and we will teach the how to's along the way.

## IT'S NOT ANOTHER FAD!

Do you find yourself following after the latest diet craze? Do you get really excited about the latest potion or pill, and are you still waiting for *Oprah* to reveal the magic cure for weight loss? Well, we have bad news. There is no magic pill and if one comes out we will probably find out a few years later that it causes cancer. What works is making little decisions every day until one day you have the health you always wanted. A lifestyle is the way, and we want to take you step by step through the process!

*Now, here is what it IS!*

## EXPERIENCE LIFE ON THE EDGE
## *FOR FREE!*

We not only want you to enjoy this cookbook; we also want to invite you to be a part of a vision bigger than yourself in *The Healthy Edge*. If you want to create an environment in your home that will change generations... If you are sick and tired of being sick and tired... If you are ready to have the health and weight release you have always wanted... If you are ready to take yourself on and experience the abundant life... You are ready for *The Healthy Edge!*

*The Healthy Edge* is a 7-week life transformation program and we want to share it with you for free for 14 days! Go to **GetTheHealthyEdge.com** and click on our Free 14-day test drive to experience it for yourself!

### *You will receive:*

• Week 1 Video on Insulin Resistance *(This alone will change your life.)*

• Week 1 Empowering Audio *(This will kick start any health journey you are beginning.)*

• Grocery and pantry lists

• 14-day meal plan

• Recipes

*and much, much more!*

# SUPPLEMENTATION

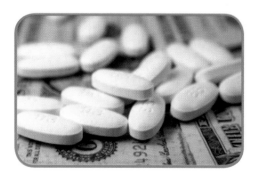

With supplements being regulated as food products and not as pharmaceuticals, there is no guarantee that what's listed on the label is in the product. Many products don't disintegrate, and can contain toxic metals, pesticides and unapproved drugs. In an unregulated industry, finding quality supplements can feel impossible. Most people sell their health to the lowest bidder and others choose to do nothing. Neither one of these scenarios will move you forward in your health.

## A TRUE STORY

Brian Thiel, Co-Founder of *The Healthy Edge*, was no stranger to supplements. Brian admits he was highly marketable and depending on what the current issue of *Men's Health* magazine was recommending, Brian was on his way to the nearest "supplement shop" to pick it up. Heading straight for the men's section, he faced endless options to choose from. Dazed and confused, he usually made a choice based on cost and label. Millions of dollars in advertising definitely works in this case.

Although Brian faithfully took his cupboard of daily supplements, he still suffered from seasonal strep throat, flu and colds that plagued him since he was a child. Although he exercised regularly and ate a healthy, balanced diet, something had to be missing. Along with the seasonal illnesses, insomnia and intestinal issues left him tired and frequently visiting specialists.

When Brian first met Amber, her passion was evident. It was one the reasons he fell in love with her so quickly. Casual conversation led to a discussion on supplementation and Amber shared her own personal journey with supplements that was inspired by her mother's battle with cancer. She had watched her mom spend thousands of dollars on products that were not providing the nutritional support her body so desperately needed. This devastating discovery was made after she had lost her mom.

Within three months of taking a pharmaceutical grade supplement, Brian was noticing a difference. His nails were growing faster and were stronger, he was sleeping restfully through the night and he noticed a difference in his workouts. After a year, his family couldn't believe that Brian survived a whole year without one bout of illness. His mom and dad were so impressed they started on a supplement as well.

## WHY SUPPLEMENT?

Brian's story is a personal testimony to the power of supplements. Our bodies are bombarded daily with stress, pollution, radiation, chemicals, and highly processed foods which causes oxidative stress in our bodies. The majority of us do not even come close to the recommended daily allowances of vitamins and minerals needed to protect our bodies. 90% of the American food budget is spent on processed food, devoid of these essential nutrients. Even a lifestyle rich in whole foods, such as fruit, vegetables, beans and nuts, contain considerably less nutrients by the time they get to our plates, due to mineral deficient soil, storage and transportation, processing and cooking. The American Medical Association now recommends that all adults take a complete multi-vitamin.

Selecting a company that follows pharmaceutical-grade Good Manufacturing Practices (GMP's) is essential in a quality supplement. These companies are expected to follow the same standards as manufacturers of over-the-counter or prescription medications. This provides you with additional assurance that what is on the label is truly in the bottle.

USP (United States Pharmacoepia) standards ensure products dissolve properly and are readily absorbed into the body. What's the point of a quality supplement if it doesn't dissolve? We encourage you to avoid "flushing" your money down the toilet with a product that does not follow USP standards.

## THE HEALTHY EDGE CRITERIA

*The Healthy Edge* does not endorse any specific company or product. This program empowers you to make your own choices about what you eat, how you move and the supplements you take. Below are some criteria in choosing a supplement that can support you in making a quality choice.

Lyle MacWilliam's book, *Nutrisearch The Comparative Guide to Nutritional Supplements 4th edition,* is a great place to start when searching for the right supplement for your family. This third-party publication provides information on how to choose a supplement and also ranks over 1500 products according to quality. Balance and completeness are addressed in this publication and are crucial in order to ensure proper absorption and interaction in your body.

## THE BOTTOM LINE

The bottom line is that supplementation, healthy eating, and moderate exercise is the tripod of health. Without any one of the three, you are unbalanced, as illustrated in Brian's health journey. Take the time to research and make a choice that is truly going to make a difference from the inside out.

When I (April) found out my daughter and I had Celiac disease and a severe sensitivity to dairy, I was scared and extremely overwhelmed. I went for weeks feeling like I couldn't eat anything and I felt extremely deprived. Then I looked up and got over feeling sorry for myself and took control of the situation.

**April & Arleena** enjoy a gluten-free life with ease!

The first step was getting educated and finding a "WHY" that was going to be strong enough to keep me away from gluten and diary. According to the Mayo Clinic staff, "Celiac disease is a digestive condition triggered by consumption of the protein gluten, which is found in bread, pasta, cookies, pizza crust and many other foods containing wheat (including durum, semolina, and spelt, barley or rye).

If you have Celiac disease and eat foods containing gluten, an immune reaction occurs in your small intestine, causing damage to the surface of your small intestine and an inability to absorb certain nutrients. Eventually, the decreased absorption of nutrients (malabsorption) that occurs with Celiac disease can cause vitamin deficiencies that deprive your brain, peripheral nervous system, bones, liver and other organs of vital nourishment. This can lead to other illnesses and stunted growth in children.

According to studies by The University of Chicago Celiac Disease Center on the prevalence of Celiac disease in the U.S., 1 in 133 average healthy people are affected. In people with front degree relatives (parent, child, sibling) who are Celiac: 1 in 22 people are affected. Because Celiac disease is hereditary, all family members should be tested if one family member is diagnosed with it.

After losing a mom to cancer there was no way that I would put myself at risk any longer by consuming gluten.

**Arleena** at the age of 5 is able to focus on everything she CAN enjoy!

Despite the horrible digestive problems I have lived with my whole life, getting off gluten and into whole foods has also allowed me to get to my optimal weight and to live without pain. From a girl that was big boned to a skinny mommy, it was all worth it!

 This cookbook contains many recipes that are marked gluten-free. Gluten-free recipes will contain the symbol shown. There is also a disclaimer that you should check with the manufacturer of any foods that are boxed, canned or may have been exposed to gluten during the storage or shipping process. The disclaimer reads: *Contact the manufacturer of this product to ensure it is gluten-free.* There are products that can contain gluten that will not be labeled as such so it is important to do your research! Did I mention I am allergic to eggs as well? There are also many recipes that are dairy and egg free, although they are not labeled. Many recipes can be modified as well to fit your particular allergy.

For people with gluten allergies, if a recipe calls for cheese (and you are not also allergic to dairy) please check the manufacturer of the cheese. You always need to check the manufacturer to assure that gluten was not added in after the cheese was processed. Many cheeses do contain gluten, so do your homework! Secondly, when using oatmeal, the package must be marked gluten-free; organic oats are not necessarily gluten-free. To ensure that you are truly eating gluten-free, check all manufacturers of any canned, boxed or bagged product you use that do not specifically say "gluten-free."

Learn more about gluten-free items for your pantry by doing our Free 14-day trial of *The Healthy Edge* program at **GetTheHealthyEdge.com**. You will be blessed with the information!

# Chicken Portobello

Makes 4 servings • Serving size: ½ Portobello mushroom & ½ chicken breast
Prep time: 15 minutes • Cook time: 1 hour

*The Healthy Edge cookbook denotes gluten-free meals by placing a gluten-free symbol in the lower-left corner of the pictures. There are also recipes that do not contain this symbol but can be prepared to be gluten-free. Refer to The Chef's Suggestions for tips on how to make dishes gluten-free!*

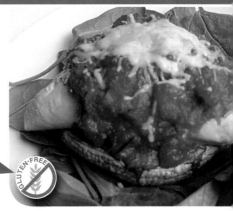

## FINDING INTERNAL MEAT TEMPERATURES

Take the dish out of the oven before checking temperature. Stick the wand (meat thermometer) into the middle of the thickest part of the meat without touching the pan or bone. When the needle has stopped moving you can read the temperature and compare to the following chart.

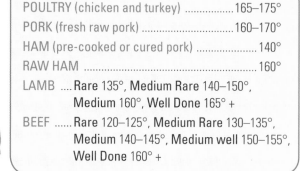

*Note:* All temperatures throughout The Healthy Edge cookbook are presented in degrees Farhrenheit.

| | |
|---|---|
| POULTRY (chicken and turkey) | 165–175° |
| PORK (fresh raw pork) | 160–170° |
| HAM (pre-cooked or cured pork) | 140° |
| RAW HAM | 160° |
| LAMB | **Rare 135°, Medium Rare 140–150°, Medium 160°, Well Done 165° +** |
| BEEF | **Rare 120–125°, Medium Rare 130–135°, Medium 140–145°, Medium well 150–155°, Well Done 160° +** |

## FISH

Fish (including seafood and crustaceans) is translucent when undercooked. It is done when color is solid and meat is flaky. Fish like tuna steaks aren't as flaky, but the meat pulls apart easily. If something like tuna stretches instead of pulls apart easily it is not well done. Some fish, like salmon and tuna, can be eaten rare as long as it is very fresh. When fish is fresh enough to eat raw or rare, it will not have a "fishy smell." Fresh fish has no distinct smell, or it may smell like cold sea water.

## HOW TO THAW FROZEN FOODS

Being prepared is not only empowering, it will make healthy living so much easier. Know what you are going to eat for the week so you can get the appropriate foods unfrozen.

Improperly thawing meats may lead to increased risk of food-borne illness, including salmonella poisoning. Some improper thawing procedures include thawing meats on the counter top, in a sink or bowl of water, under running water, and in the microwave.

To properly thaw meats, pull from freezer and place in a bowl or on a plate and place on bottom shelf in the refrigerator. (This will keep things clean if there is any leakage.) Many large cuts of meat will take longer than 24 hours to thaw. Do not try to cook frozen meat; wait until it is thawed completely. Here are some examples of the time it may take to thaw some cuts of meat (times may vary due to fridge and freezer temps).

| | |
|---|---|
| 4-6 oz. FISH FILLETS | *12–24 hours* |
| 6 oz. CHICKEN BREASTS | *12–24 hours* |
| PORK TENDERLOIN | *18–36 hours* |
| BEEF ROAST *(2 lbs)* | *18–36 hours* |
| WHOLE CHICKEN | *2–3 days* |
| WHOLE TURKEY *(16-20 lbs)* | *up to 1 week* |

# HOW TO PROLONG THE LIFE OF YOUR PRODUCE

## Lettuces

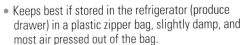

- Wash and spin dry.
- Store cut or whole leaves in air tight container.
- Keeps best if stored in the refrigerator (produce drawer) in a plastic zipper bag, slightly damp, and most air pressed out of the bag.
- Will stay fresh for 7–10 days.

> *TIP: After washing and spinning, place on a paper towel to air dry. The lettuce will still be slightly damp for storage. Cut lettuce will brown more quickly than whole leaf lettuce like spring mix or arugula.*

## Root vegetables
*(Carrots, beets, turnips, Jerusalem artichokes)*

- Wash and air dry for several hours.
- Store in plastic zipper bags in the refrigerator.
- Will stay fresh for up to several weeks when stored completely dry.

## Fruits, Whole Firm
*(Apples, pears, peaches, plums, nectarines)*

- Last longest when washed and stored in the refrigerator produce drawer (instead of in a fruit bowl).
- Keep fruits and vegetables separate. Many types of fruits emit ethylene gas, which can accelerate the ripening of vegetables stored nearby. This is why there are typically two separate drawers (crispers) in most refrigerators.

## Grapes and Cherries

- Wash and remove grapes from the stems.
- To keep them longer, store in a glass (or BPA-free plastic) container with a lid after washing.
- For homes with children, after washing we suggest storing them in the refrigerator in a bowl. Kids can grab a handful of grapes as a snack when they are hungry.

## Bananas, Avocados, Onions, Garlic, Sweet Potatoes/Yams, Fall Harvest Squash

- All store well in a fruit bowl on the counter top, or in a well ventilated area.
- Some of these items can be prone to mold if stored in a congested area.

## Summer Squash, Zucchini, Broccoli, Cauliflower, Peppers, Asparagus, Legumes *(i.e. Green Beans)*

- Wash and air dry completely.
- Store in an air-tight container or zipper bag in the refrigerator produce drawer.

> *TIP: Cut broccoli and cauliflower before placing in bags to make quick grab snacks. All other veggies store longest if whole.*
>
> *Julienne-slice peppers and place in baggies for quick snacks, but they are only good for about 2 days when cut.*

## Tomatoes

- Best stored at room temperature and used up while fresh.
- Cut tomatoes should be stored in an air-tight container in the refrigerator.

## Herbs
*(rosemary, thyme, oregano, etc.)*

- Trim the bottoms and put the stems in water. Loosely cover with a plastic bag and place in the refrigerator.
- Be sure to change the water daily to prolong freshness.
- Store basil the same way (but without plastic bag covering) on the countertop as long as it's not too hot.
- Basil can be stored in the least cold spot of the refrigerator. When it is stored too cold, the leaves will turn black.

## TEN POUNDS A YEAR ADDS UP

**ABOUT THREE YEARS AGO, I STARTED TO GAIN ABOUT 10 POUNDS A YEAR.** I remember being told that this is what happens after you hit thirty years, so I justified it. The realization that I needed to do something was when I got my blood markers back in April of 2008 and my cholesterol and triglycerides were really high and my blood pressure was through the roof. I had to do something.

When I graduated, my wife and I decided to buckle down and really get serious about our health. Since we were eating healthily, or so I thought because of what I learned in my single nutrition class in college, I was determined that we just needed to move more.

**BEFORE**

We joined a gym in January 2009. We worked out at least five days a week and I burned 700 calories a day and at the end of the first month I had lost about 6 pounds. At that rate I figured it would take me until around the end of June to reach my goal weight of 180 pounds.

This was my plan until my wife learned about *The Healthy Edge* lifestyle program. She dragged me to the introductory seminar. While she was excited to get started, I still felt I knew everything I needed to know due to my Health Enhancement degree. I decided to support her and participate in the program.

**AFTER**

We implemented *The Healthy Edge* lifestyle with a 100% conviction, and I had reached my goal weight, three months earlier than what I had estimated. Since beginning *The Healthy Edge*, I have released over 49 pounds, 13 pounds beyond my initial goal. I began at 26% body fat and now I am at 15%, which is average for men, and my blood pressure is within normal range. At 32, I feel healthier than I did when I was in high school! Thank you *Healthy Edge*!

## Michael Weideman, USA
**RELEASED 49 POUNDS AND 11% BODY FAT**

**I HAVE STRUGGLED WITH WEIGHT MY WHOLE LIFE, BUT IT WAS BECOMING MORE THAN JUST A WEIGHT CONCERN.** I was having trouble with high blood pressure and then began experiencing low blood sugar. When I would eat what I thought was somewhat healthy food, I would be hungry in a couple hours. I was also very light-headed and shaky. I would feel faint and get very irritable. When I did eat, I couldn't stop eating until I felt better.

I was scared, and always frustrated and disgusted with myself. In January, when I went in for a checkup, I knew I needed to tell someone about this problem. I had gained 90 pounds in 2½ years and I had had enough. I was informed that it sounded like I had spiked my blood sugar one too many times. That same night there was an opportunity to learn about a lifestyle program that could address what I was dealing with. The timing couldn't have been better; I knew I had to do this. So I went.

**BEFORE**

I was so excited about the information I had heard. Since I started implementing *The Healthy Edge* lifestyle, I have not once experienced the light-headed spells that I so often had experienced. I want to go to the gym, because I feel good about myself when I do. I have released more than 85 pounds, and am always looking for ways to be active. I used to have trouble with my lower back and my feet hurting constantly. And now, I am pain free.

I have yet to reach my goal, but then again, I don't really feel like I need a goal anymore because I'm going to continue living *The Healthy Edge* no matter what. As long as my body needs to release fat, it will.

*The Healthy Edge* has been the best thing ever for my husband and me. It has completely changed our lives. We plan on starting a family soon and this was huge motivation for us throughout the entire journey. We can't wait to be able to provide healthy food for our children and have the energy to keep up with them.

**AFTER**

*The Healthy Edge* is different from anything else out there! We supported one another and were able to keep each other on track. We have also reached out with this knowledge to many of our family, friends, and co-workers, which has been incredibly fulfilling. This truly is a lifestyle and we are excited to live it every day.

Brittney Weideman, USA • **RELEASED 85 POUNDS**

# Berry Good Oatmeal

Makes 2 servings
Serving size: 1 cup
Total time: 20 minutes

 **What you'll need:**

1 cup organic skim milk *(substitute water if preparing dairy free)*

1 cup water

1 cup whole oats*

1 pinch sea salt

1 tsp pure vanilla extract *(alcohol free)*

⅛ tsp cinnamon

½ cup fresh or frozen organic berries *(blackberries, strawberries, and/or blueberries)*

1. Combine milk and water together in a medium saucepan over high heat.

2. As the milk or water begins to boil, stir in oats and salt.

3. Reduce heat to medium-low and cook for 10 minutes.

4. Stir in vanilla and cinnamon, cook for another 5–7 minutes until the desired consistency is reached.

5. Stir in fresh (or frozen) berries.

6. Divide into two bowls and serve immediately.

   *Contact manufacturer to ensure product is gluten-free.*

 **Chef's Serving Suggestions**

- To make an apple cinnamon variation of this oatmeal, stir in 1 diced organic apple with step #4, and 1/2 cup raisins instead of berries in step #5.

- You can substitute ½ cup unsweetened organic applesauce with the raisins instead of using diced apples.

- To make creamier oatmeal, soak the oats for 1–8 hours before cooking.

- You can also combine water, milk, and oats into a pot and soak overnight in the refrigerator. In the morning, add vanilla, cinnamon and salt. Cook on medium heat for about 15–20 minutes, stirring occasionally.

- Make this with any combination of milk and water as long as 2 cups of liquid is used. Adding just that little bit of skim milk gives the oatmeal a whole different flavor than if you prepare it with water alone.

# Banana Pecan Buckwheat Pancakes

Makes about 10 pancakes or 4–5 waffles
Serving size: 2 pancake or ½ waffle
Total time: 15–20 minutes

## What you'll need:

2 bananas

½ cup low-fat plain organic yogurt

2 organic eggs

½ cup soy flour

½ cup buckwheat flour *(stone ground preferred)*\*

½ tsp baking soda

1 tsp baking powder

1 cup organic skim milk

½ cup raw, unsalted pecans, coarsely chopped

½ tsp olive oil or cooking spray

*\*See Chef's Suggestions for gluten-free grains.*

1. Peel bananas and mash in a bowl with a potato masher. Bananas will become creamy. You can leave some chunks of banana too.

2. Add eggs and yogurt. Mix well with a spatula or wooden spoon.

3. In a separate bowl, combine dry ingredients.

4. Add the dry ingredients to the banana mixture and stir well.

5. Add milk until a smooth consistency is reached, stir in pecans last.

6. Heat a non-stick pan over medium heat.

7. Coat the pan with olive oil cooking spray or a small amount of olive oil. Ladle ⅓ of a cup of batter into the pan for each pancake.

8. The key to cooking pancakes is slow and easy. Wait until the batter begins to bubble and they are solid enough to flip with a spatula. This takes about 4–5 minutes on the first side and approximately 2 minutes on the other side.

###  Chef's Serving Suggestions

- You can substitute 100% stone ground whole wheat flour or 100% stone ground whole wheat pastry flour.

- This recipe can be *gluten-free* if you use gluten-free flour such as amaranth, buckwheat, brown rice or quinoa flour.

- Use raw agave nectar, real fruit preserves with no added sugar, real maple syrup or yogurt as a topping.

- To make waffles use 3/4–1 cup of batter in a Belgium waffle maker per waffle. Leaving the waffle in too long will cause it to become dry. Waffles are done when they don't stick to the waffle maker.

- Serve with some fresh fruit and eggs for a complete breakfast.

- Remember, these are a healthier version of pancakes and waffles, but are not recommended everyday for a *Healthy Edge* lifestyle.

# Buckwheat Banana Bread

Makes 1 loaf, about 10–12 slices
Serving size: 1 slice • Prep time: 15 minutes
Cook time: 45–50 minutes

 ## What you'll need:

3 bananas

3 carrots, peeled and grated

2 organic eggs

¼ cup olive oil

¼ cup raw agave nectar

½ cup organic unsweetened
   apple sauce

1 cup 100% whole wheat pastry
   flour *(stone ground preferred)**

1 cup 100% whole buckwheat flour
   *(stone ground preferred)**

¼ cup flax seed meal

2 tsp baking soda

1 tsp baking powder

1 tsp ground cinnamon

½ tsp ground nutmeg

¾ cup raw, unsalted walnuts, coarsely chopped

1 tsp olive oil or coconut oil or olive oil spray

---

 ### Chef's Serving Suggestions

- This recipe can be gluten-free if you use gluten-free flour such as amaranth, buckwheat, brown rice or quinoa flour.

- Slice as needed, bread will remain freshest this way.

- Store in an airtight container for up to 4 days.

- This bread can be frozen. Allow it to thaw on counter top for a day before slicing.

- Toast each slice in the toaster and spread it with your favorite raw, unsalted nut butter.

- This recipe is a treat to have with breakfast. It is also a nice surprise for children if you pack a slice in their lunch box.

- In addition to the carrots, you could add ½ cup shredded zucchini.

---

1. Preheat oven to 350° and spray inside of loaf pan with non-stick olive oil cooking spray or rub with olive oil or coconut oil.

2. Mash bananas in a bowl with a potato masher.

3. Stir in all other ingredients in order listed, making sure each is well combined before adding the next.

4. Pour batter into prepared loaf pan and bake for 45 minutes to 1 hour.

5. At 45 minutes, insert a toothpick into the center. If it comes out clean, the bread is done. If not, check in 5 more minutes. Do not let it cook past 1 hour, or you will have dry bread!

6. Allow bread to cool in pan on cooling rack for 5 minutes before turning it over and removing from pan.

7. Allow bread to cool completely on cooling rack before slicing. Good luck letting it cool down before serving!

*See Chef's Suggestions for gluten-free grains.*

# 1 Plus 2 Scramble

Makes 1 serving
Total time: 10 minutes

## What you'll need:

1 organic egg

2 organic egg whites

1 Tbsp diced organic tomatoes

1 Tbsp diced organic bell peppers

1 Tbsp diced red onions

2 Tbsp organic spinach

1 Tbsp organic feta cheese*

1 tsp olive oil or cooking spray

1. Place an 8" omelet pan on medium-high heat. Spray lightly with olive oil cooking spray or add 1 tsp olive oil.

2. Whisk eggs together until well combined.

3. Mix in all other ingredients.

4. Pour into hot pan and scramble until they reach your desired style.

   *Contact manufacturer to ensure product is gluten-free.*

### Chef's Serving Suggestions

- Serve these scramblers with fresh fruit for a complete meal.
- Be creative and use a variety of vegetables.

# Egg White Garden Omelet

Makes 1 omelet
Total prep time: 15 minutes

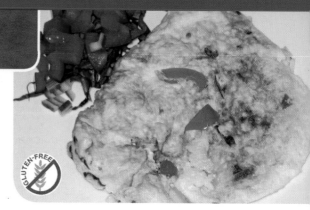

 **What you'll need:**

4 organic egg whites

¼ cup organic skim milk

1 Tbsp diced organic tomatoes

1 Tbsp diced organic red bell peppers

1 Tbsp diced red onion

1 Tbsp low fat organic cheese*

2 Tbsp fresh organic spinach, chopped

1 tsp of olive oil or cooking spray

**OMELET INGREDIENTS**

1. Place an 8" or 10" omelet pan on medium high heat.

2. Spray lightly with olive oil cooking spray or add 1 tsp of olive oil. If you are using a really good non-stick pan, you won't need to use anything.

3. Whisk the egg whites until they begin to froth and are well combined.

4. Whisk in the milk.

5. Add all other ingredients and mix together with a whisk or fork.

6. Pour the mixture into the hot pan and reduce heat to just above medium.

7. Flip over when the eggs are cooked throughout and solid enough not to tear. (After about 5–7 minutes)

8. Cook another 3–5 minutes. Omelet is ready to serve.

*Contact manufacturer to ensure product is gluten-free.*

 **Chef's Serving Suggestions**

- This omelet is great without using salt, pepper, or any other seasoning. If you choose, you can add some fresh thyme or fresh cracked black pepper for added flavor.

# Fiesta Quiche

Makes 6 servings
Prep time: 10 minutes
Cook time: 30 minutes

## What you'll need:

6 large organic eggs

1½ cup low-fat organic milk

¼ cup 100% whole wheat flour *(stone ground preferred)*\*

½ red onion, chopped

½ each red and green organic bell peppers, finely chopped

½ cup mushrooms, chopped

½ cup organic spinach, chopped

½ cup organic diced tomatoes *(seeds removed optional)*

½ fresh jalapeno, minced *(seeds removed)*

3 oz. shredded organic cheddar cheese\*\*

½ tsp sea salt

½ tsp black pepper

1 tsp olive oil or coconut oil or olive oil spray

## Chef's Serving Suggestions

- Double the recipe and bake in a 13"x9" dish.
- This recipe can be made gluten-free if you use a gluten-free flour such as amaranth, buckwheat, brown rice or quinoa flour.
- Serve quiche with oatmeal, organic yogurt, fresh organic fruit or sliced avocado for a complete breakfast.
- Quiche can be prepared the night before and stored covered in the fridge. Remove from fridge as you pre-heat the oven and bake as directed.
- This is a great breakfast for the holiday season and when you are entertaining guests.

1. Preheat oven to 400°. Spray a 9" pie plate with olive oil cooking spray or rub with olive oil or coconut oil.

2. Wisk together eggs, milk, and flour until well combined. (You can place all three in a food processor or blender for a quick mix.)

3. Stir remaining ingredients into the egg mixture.

4. Pour mixture into prepared pie plate and bake 30 minutes or until a knife inserted in the center comes out clean.

5. Cool for 5–10 minutes. Cut into 6 slices and serve.

*\*See Chef's serving Suggestions for gluten-free grains.*

*\*\*Contact manufacturer to ensure product is gluten-free.*

# Mediterranean Quiche

Makes 6 servings
Prep time: 10 minutes
Cook time: 30 minutes

 **What you'll need:**

6 large organic eggs

1½ cup low-fat organic milk

¼ cup 100% whole wheat flour *(stone ground preferred)*\*

½ red onion, chopped

1 red organic red bell pepper, finely chopped

½ cup organic spinach, chopped

½ cup organic tomatoes, diced *(seeds removed optional)*

3 oz. crumbled organic feta cheese\*\*

½ tsp sea salt

½ tsp black pepper

1 tsp olive oil or coconut oil or olive oil cooking spray

① Preheat oven to 400°. Spray a 9" pie plate with olive oil cooking spray or rub with olive oil or coconut oil.

② Wisk together eggs, milk, and flour until well combined. Use a food processor to save time.

③ Stir remaining ingredients into the egg mixture.

④ Pour mixture into prepared pie plate and bake 30 minutes or until a knife inserted in the center comes out clean.

⑤ Cool for 5–10 minutes then cut into 6 slices and serve.

*\*See Chef's Suggestions for gluten-free grains.*

*\*\*Contact manufacturer to ensure product is gluten-free.*

 **Chef's Serving Suggestions**

- Serve quiche with oatmeal, yogurt, fresh fruit, or ½ avocado for a complete breakfast.

- This recipe can be gluten-free if you use gluten-free flour such as amaranth, buckwheat, brown rice or quinoa.

- This is great for the holiday season and when you are entertaining guests.

- You can use 3 large eggs combined with 4 or 5 egg whites to save on saturated fat and cholesterol content.

- Quiche can be prepared the night before and stored covered in fridge. Remove from fridge as you pre-heat the oven then bake as directed.

# Brunch Quiche

Makes 6 servings
Prep time: 10–15 minutes
Cook time: 30 minutes

## What you'll need:

6 large organic eggs

1½ cup organic low-fat milk

¼ cup 100% whole wheat flour *(stone ground preferred)*\*

½ red onion, chopped

1 cup broccoli florets, chopped

½ cup shredded carrots

½ cup browned lean ground organic turkey

4 oz. shredded organic cheddar cheese\*\*

½ tsp sea salt

½ tsp black pepper

1 tsp olive oil or coconut oil or olive oil spray

### Chef's Serving Suggestions

- Double the recipe and bake in a 13"x 9" dish.

- This recipe can be gluten-free if you use gluten-free flour such as amaranth, buckwheat, brown rice or quinoa flour.

- Use 3 large eggs and 4 or 5 egg whites instead of 6 eggs.

- Quiche can be prepared the night before and stored covered in fridge. Remove from fridge as you pre-heat the oven then bake as directed.

1. Preheat oven to 400°. Spray a 9" pie plate with olive oil cooking spray or rub with olive oil or coconut oil.

2. Wisk together eggs, milk, and flour until well combined. Use a food processor to save time.

3. Stir remaining ingredients into the egg mixture.

4. Pour mixture into prepared pie plate and bake 30 minutes or until a knife inserted in the center comes out clean.

5. Cool for 5–10 minutes. Cut into 6 slices and serve.

*\*See Chef's Suggestions for gluten-free grains.*

*\*\*Contact manufacturer to ensure product is gluten-free.*

# Veggie Overload Quiche

Makes 6 servings
Prep time: 10 minutes
Cook time: 30 minutes

## What you'll need:

7 large organic eggs

1½ cup low-fat organic milk

¼ cup 100% whole wheat flour
*(stone ground preferred)**

½ red onion, chopped

1 cup broccoli florets, chopped

½ cup mushrooms, chopped

½ cup fresh organic spinach, chopped

½ cup fresh organic diced tomatoes *(seeds removed)*

½ each organic red and green bell peppers, diced

½ cup shredded carrots

½ cup shredded zucchini

4 oz. shredded cheddar cheese

½ tsp sea salt

½ tsp black pepper

1 tsp olive oil or coconut oil or olive oil cooking spray

## Chef's Serving Suggestions

- You can use 3 large eggs combined with 4 or 5 egg whites.

- This recipe can be made gluten-free if you use gluten-free flour such as amaranth, buckwheat, brown rice or quinoa.

- Quiche can be prepared the night before and stored covered in fridge. Remove from fridge as you pre-heat the oven then bake as directed.

1. Preheat oven to 400°. Spray a 13"x 9" pie plate with olive oil cooking spray or rub with olive oil or coconut oil.

2. Wisk together eggs, milk, and flour until well combined. Use a food processor to save time.

3. Stir remaining ingredients into the egg mixture.

4. Pour mixture into prepared pie plate and bake 30 minutes or until a knife inserted in the center comes out clean.

5. Cool for 5–10 minutes then cut into 6 slices and serve.

*See Chef's Suggestions for gluten-free grains.*

*You won't believe there's spinach in this smoothie!*

# Arleena's Super Smoothie

Makes two 8 oz. smoothies
Serving size 8 oz.
Total time: 5–10 minutes

## What you'll need:

14 oz. coconut milk, almond milk, or water

7 ice cubes

1½ cups organic baby spinach

½ avocado

1 small organic apple *(sweeter the better)*

1 banana

2 heaping Tbsp high quality protein or 1 heaping Tbsp of meal replacement powder*

1 heaping Tbsp ground flaxseed

2 Tbsp organic peanut butter

Agave nectar to taste *(if desired)*

1 Wash spinach and apple.

2 Cut banana and apple into small pieces (be sure to remove seeds from apple).

3 Measure out 14 oz. of liquid and put all ingredients into the blender. Blend until smooth with no chunks.

4 Taste and add agave nectar or additional fruit to taste.

5 Serve immediately.

*Contact manufacturer to ensure product is gluten-free..*

### Chef's Serving Suggestions

• This is Arleena's favorite breakfast, she requests it almost everyday. April and Arleena enjoy using different fruits with the same combinations of other ingredients to make a variety of healthy and very tasty morning smoothies.

• Add ½ of a red beet (washed, peeled and chopped) to your shake to change the color from green to a fruity looking masterpiece for your children.

• Children need the quality calories in this smoothie. What a great way to get a lot of nutrition in their bodies to start the day!

• If making for your children, don't let them watch you put the ingredients together if they are picky eaters. They will love the taste and they won't even know it's good for them!

• Feel free to substitute your favorite fruits! Mangos, strawberries, and whatever else you have around the house will go great in this smoothie. The combination of spinach and avocado are perfectly masked when mixed with most sweet fruits!

• If you desire a sweeter smoothie add agave nectar to taste. Feel free to play with this to find your perfect healthy combination that will become your new favorite breakfast.

• The Healthy Edge has recommendations for purchasing protein and meal replacement shakes. Reading food labels on these products is very important due to artificial sweeteners and colors that are present in most store bought products.

## CHANGE YOUR MIND, CHANGE YOUR LIFE

**THE HEALTHY EDGE HAS CHANGED MY LIFE IN SO MANY WAYS.** At 63, I started *The Healthy Edge* because of my daughter, Wendy. She wanted me to live longer and be healthy. I guess you can't go wrong with that way of thinking. I had no expectations of what I would get out of this. I released 57.5 pounds and I learned so much.

**BEFORE**

I had done a bunch of fad diets in my lifetime. What was missing was I never addressed or changed my way of thinking. I have finally accepted that I was overweight because of me. I fully realized that I am responsible for myself and no one else. I started choosing to eat healthily and exercising more. I used the recipes from *The Healthy Edge* website and they actually tasted good. I mean, REALLY good.

With what I learned in *The Healthy Edge* and the new recipes, I was off. I started releasing weight and I was full all the time. My favorite saying I learned from the class was, "This isn't your last meal." I didn't have to stuff myself because I will be eating again in a couple of hours. Well, that sure worked for me.

**AFTER**

When I lost some weight, people asked what I was doing. Most of the people did not want to make changes, but I did. They wanted to get results without doing anything. How does that happen? I feel better. I look better. On the inside, I am getting stronger, healthier and I am more positive. How great is that?

In the program, I learned and fully realized that I could choose to be around people who make me feel good and not ones that try to take me down or make me feel bad. *The Healthy Edge* taught me about how to be strong and positive and feel good about myself. The weight release is a bonus!

Thanks!

Gail Kesler, USA
**RELEASED 57.5 POUNDS**

**MY LIFE BEFORE THE HEALTHY EDGE WAS OUT OF CONTROL!** I ate when and what I wanted, and then I ate too much of the wrong food choices. I felt guilty and ate more. It was a vicious cycle which made my self respect go out the window. Along with feeling fat, I also felt stupid and ugly. These feelings made me hard to live with. High blood pressure has been a problem of mine and extra weight didn't help.

Change isn't easy for me, especially because I truly enjoy eating. I had done weight loss programs with some success but I always found my way back to unhealthy food and hence the weight returned. I was determined this time that I would lose the weight for good. What I didn't realize was that I would not only "release" weight but I would also gain confidence. I feel better about myself than I have for a long time. Thank you Healthy Edge!

**BEFORE**

*The Healthy Edge* not only changed my life, but my transformation has had an impact on my family as well. Our children are grown but my husband and I are now eating in a healthy way and feeling better emotionally and physically. Our attitudes have changed. Mine is much more positive and I feel I can handle problems more easily. I am also NEVER hungry.

**AFTER**

There has been some times when I've craved snacks that aren't healthy. I have broken down and eaten them, but then I feel sick. It's my body saying, "I don't like this food any more, give me healthy, good food." I believe this is probably the best present I've given myself with *The Healthy Edge*. My body actually knows the difference between healthy and unhealthy. This is a wonderful journey and I'm in it for the long haul.

Thank you Healthy Edge!

LuAnn Servo, USA
**RELEASED 20 POUNDS**

# Hummus

Makes 3 cups • Serving size: ½ cup
Prep time: 1 hour 10 minutes (largely unattended)
or see quick prep (10 minutes) below

 **What you'll need:**

1 cup dried garbanzo beans *(chick peas)*

1½ Tbsp minced garlic

2 tsp fresh thyme, chopped

2 tsp fresh rosemary, chopped

1/3 cup fresh chives, minced

2/3 cup low-sodium chicken stock*

½ cup organic tomatoes, diced

1 cup loosely packed fresh grated organic
   Parmesan cheese* *(optional)*

1. Soak beans overnight. Drain.

2. Bring beans to boil in a pot of
   water or low sodium chicken
   stock.

3. Reduce heat to medium and cook
   until tender, approximately 1 hour.

4. Drain beans through a colander
   and combine while hot in
   food processor with all other
   ingredients, except the parmesan
   cheese.

5. Pulse until thoroughly combined.
   Add cheese and pulse again.
   Hummus should be smooth and
   not chunky.

   *Contact manufacturer to ensure product
   is gluten-free.*

 **Chef's Serving Suggestions**

- To make this quickly, you can use 2 cans
  low-sodium garbanzo beans*, drained.

- The Parmesan cheese gives this hummus
  a creamy texture and adds flavor. If you
  choose to leave out the cheese, add in ½
  tsp sea salt. This would also make this
  recipe dairy free.

- Serve immediately while warm or cover and
  refrigerate up to 4 days. Hummus can be
  served chilled or at room temperature.

- Serve with raw veggies.

- Use as a spread for your wrap or sandwich.

- Use as creative topping for taco night or
  serve with home baked tortilla or 100%
  whole grain pita chips. There are endless
  uses for this great dip. The kids LOVE it!

# Black Olive Hummus

Makes 3 cups • Serving size: ¼ cup
Prep time: 1 hour 5 minutes (largely unattended)
or see quick prep (15 minutes) below

 **What you'll need:**

1 cup dried garbanzo beans *(soaked in water 8–24 hours)*

1/3 cup red onions, minced

½ cup pitted black olives

1 cup fresh grated organic Parmesan cheese*

2 cloves (or 2 tsp) garlic, minced

2/3 cup low-sodium chicken stock*

6 fresh basil leaves, chopped

1 organic Roma tomato, diced

½ tsp sea salt

1. Cook the garbanzo beans. Drain the water they soaked in, add to a pot, fill with fresh water and bring to a boil. Reduce heat to medium and simmer for 1 hour.

2. Drain garbanzo beans and blend with all other ingredients in a food processor for about 1 minute. Serve.

   *Contact manufacturer to ensure product is gluten-free.*

 **Chef's Serving Suggestions**

- To make this quickly, use 2 cans (15 oz) low-sodium garbanzo beans,* drained.
- Serve with veggies!
- Use it as a spread or dip on 100% whole grain crackers or on a sandwich.
- It's so good you can eat it with a spoon!

# Bay & Basil Hummus

Makes 3 cups • Serving size: ¼ cup
Prep time: 1 hour 10 minutes (largely unattended)
or see quick prep (10 minutes) below

 **What you'll need:**

1 cup dried garbanzo beans *(soaked in water 8–24 hours)*

4 bay leaves

½ cup red onions, minced

2/3 cup fresh grated organic Parmesan cheese*

1 clove garlic, minced *(or 1 tsp)*

2/3 cup low-sodium chicken stock*

6 fresh basil leaves, chopped

¼ tsp sea salt

❶ Cook the garbanzo beans. Drain the water they soaked in. Add to a pot of fresh water and bay leaves and bring to a boil.

❷ Reduce heat to medium and simmer for 1 hour.

❸ Drain garbanzo beans and blend with all other ingredients in a food processor for about 1 minute.

❹ Ready to serve.

*Contact manufacturer to ensure product is gluten-free.

 **Chef's Serving Suggestions**

- To make this quickly, you can use 2 cans low-sodium garbanzo beans,* drained.
- This dip is so good with veggies, as a spread or eat it with a spoon!!
- Great Healthy Edge snack! Loaded with protein and fiber.

Makes 2¼ cups • Serving size: ¼ cup
Total time: 5 minutes

## What you'll need:

1 cup garbanzo beans *(pre-cooked or canned, drained and rinsed)*\*

1 Tbsp red onions, minced

1 avocado *(skin and pit removed)*

12 pitted black olives *(optional)*

1 clove fresh garlic, minced

1 organic Roma tomato, chopped

4 Tbsp low-sodium chicken stock\*

1 tsp sea salt

2 oz. crumbled organic feta cheese\*

1. Combine all ingredients together in a food processor and blend until just combined.

2. Ready to serve.

*\*Contact manufacturer to ensure product is gluten-free.*

### Chef's Serving Suggestions

• Serve as a dip for veggies or 100% whole grain pita chips.

• Use as a spread on wraps, sandwiches, or pita pockets.

# Perfect Party Vegetable Dip

Makes 1¾ cup
Serving size: ¼ cup with veggies
Total time: 10 minutes

 **What you'll need:**

½ cup fresh organic spinach, chopped

½ cup low-sodium canned artichoke hearts*

¼ cup low-sodium roasted red peppers*

1 tsp fresh thyme, chopped *(1/2 tsp dried)*

1 tsp fresh garlic, minced

1 Tbsp plus 2 tsp red onion, diced

½ cup low-fat organic ricotta cheese*

½ cup low-fat organic cottage cheese*

¼ tsp sea salt

❶ Mix all ingredients together in a food processor for about 30 seconds to 1 minute or until it reaches desired consistency.

*Contact manufacturer to ensure product is gluten-free.*

 **Chef's Serving Suggestions**

- This dip is great served with fresh vegetables, 100% stone ground crackers, or 100% whole grain pita chips.
- Spread on sandwiches and wraps instead of mayonnaise.
- A favorite and fun dipper is fresh asparagus!

# Pico de Gallo

Makes 1 cup
Total time: 15 minutes or less

## What you'll need:

2 organic Roma tomatoes, diced

¼ cup onion, minced

2 cloves fresh garlic, minced

2 tsp fresh cilantro, chopped

3 Tbsp white wine vinegar* or white
   Balsamic vinegar*

1 Tbsp extra-virgin olive oil

¼ tsp sea salt

**1** Stir all ingredients together and serve immediately or refrigerate.

**2** Ready to serve!

*Contact manufacturer to ensure product is gluten-free.*

### Chef's Serving Suggestions

- Serve on 100% stone ground or sprouted grain crackers or 100% whole grain pumpernickel bread for a quick appetizer.

- Use as a salad topper.

- Use as a dip for baked tortilla chips or 100% whole grain pita chips.

- Serve on tacos, burritos, or fajitas.

- Use in a pita, wrap, or sandwich.

# Avocado & Black Bean Salsa

Makes 5 servings
Serving size: ½ cup
Prep time: 10 minutes

 **What you'll need:**

2 organic Roma tomatoes, diced

¾ cup black beans* *(canned or pre-cooked)*

½ cup whole kernel corn* *(canned or pre-cooked)*

½ cup red onion, diced small

5 stems of fresh cilantro, stripped and chopped

1 Tbsp extra-virgin olive oil

¼ tsp sea salt *(optional)*

1 avocado, diced *(skin and pit removed)*

1 Mix all ingredients together except avocado.

2 Gently stir in avocado last. Over-stirring will make avocado mushy and pasty instead of chunky.

*\*Contact manufacturer to ensure product is gluten-free.*

 **Chef's Serving Suggestions**

- Serve immediately or chill. Eat this wonderful salsa within a day or two for maximum freshness and taste.
- Begin with chilled ingredients (especially avocado) to help maintain the avocado chunks.
- Serve with some home-baked tortilla chips or on small 100% whole grain pumpernickel squares as a hors d'oeuvre.
- Serve it on salads, fajitas, or wraps.
- Eat this simply as is!

# Salsa Verde

Makes 2 cups
Serving size: 2 Tbsp
Total time: 10 minutes

 **What you'll need:**

2 cups tomatillos, cubed *(about 6–7 tomatillos needed)*

1 Tbsp fresh garlic, minced

¼ red onion, minced

1 tsp extra-virgin olive oil

¼ tsp sea salt

**GLUTEN-FREE**

**TOMATILLOS** resemble small green tomatoes wrapped in a papery husk. Tomatillos have a lemony flavor that's pleasantly tart when raw and mellow when cooked.

*Substitute:* green tomatoes with a dash of fresh lemon juice

1. Combine all ingredients together in a food processor.

2. Ready to serve!

 **Chef's Serving Suggestions**

- This is a bit on the spicy side, but so tasty!
- Use this as a salsa dip, a topping for tacos or fajitas, or on salads.
- You can stir in an additional ¼ red onion (diced) and 2 organic Roma tomatoes (diced) for a chunky salsa or topping.

# Smoked Salmon Tar-tar on Pumpernickel

Makes 15 servings
Serving size: 1 Tbsp
Prep time: 10–15 minutes

## What you'll need:

1 cup wild smoked salmon, chopped

2 Tbsp red onion, minced

1 Tbsp fresh dill, chopped

2 tsp extra-virgin olive oil

¼ cup fresh lemon juice

Fresh dill sprigs *(optional)*

2–3 Tbsp organic low-fat organic cottage cheese or Greek style yogurt *(optional)*

100% whole grain pumpernickel bread

① Stir together all ingredients.

② Serve on 2"x 2" squares of 100% whole grain pumpernickel bread.

③ Garnish with fresh dill and a tiny dollop of organic low-fat organic cottage cheese or Greek style yogurt if desired.

 **Chef's Serving Suggestions**

• Fresh sushi-grade salmon can be substituted and served raw.

• This is a great party appetizer as is or serve 1 Tbsp on a thick slice of cucumber or on an endive leaf.

# Bruschetta

Makes 10 appetizer servings
Serving size: 1 Tbsp each
Total prep time: 5–10 minutes

## What you'll need:

1 organic Roma tomato *(cut in half, remove seeds, and cut into small squares)*

2 tsp red onion, minced

1 tsp fresh basil, finely chopped

2 tsp olive oil

1 tsp Balsamic vinegar

1 pinch sea salt

**1** Mix Together.

## To make crostinis:

Take sourdough bread and slice thinly. Cut into bite-size pieces if desired (2"x 2" squares). Brush on a small amount of olive oil and toast in the oven on a baking sheet at 400° until golden brown. Remove from oven and transfer from baking sheet to cooling rack. You can serve immediately or allow crostinis to completely cool. Store in an airtight container for up to 3 days.

## Chef's Serving Suggestions

- This is great with 2 oz. organic feta cheese, crumbled. (Not if you have a dairy allergy!)
- Add ¼ cup diced artichoke hearts for a tasty variation!
- To make gluten-free, skip the crackers and crostinis and serve on sliced cucumbers.
- Serve on 100% whole grain crackers (see list of crackers in *The Healthy Edge Kids* section of the cookbook), toasted 100% whole grain pumpernickel, sourdough crostinis, or 100% whole grain baked pita chips.

# Guacamole for Two

Makes 2 servings
Total prep time: 5–10 minutes

 **What you'll need:**

1 avocado *(skin and pit removed)*

1½ tsp red onion, chopped

1 clove fresh garlic, chopped

1½ tsp fresh cilantro, chopped

¼ tsp sea salt

½ organic Roma tomato, cubed
*(about 1/3 cup)*

❶ Stir together avocado, onion, garlic, cilantro, and sea salt until well combined and creamy.

❷ Stir in tomato.

❸ Ready to serve!

 **Chef's Serving Suggestions**

- Use this guacamole as a dip for veggies, 100% stone ground tortilla chips or 100% whole grain pita chips.
- Spread on wraps or use instead of mayo on sandwiches.
- Use as a topping on your salad instead of salad dressing. Now that's living *The Healthy Edge!*

# Olive Tapenade

Makes 6 servings
Serving size: about 1 Tbsp
Prep Time: 5 minutes

 **What you'll need:**

½ cup Kalamata olives, pitted*

3 Tbsp onions, chopped

1 tsp fresh garlic, chopped

1 tsp fresh chives or parsley, chopped

# Marinated Olives

Makes 10 servings
Serving size: 2 olives
Prep time: 5 minutes

## What you'll need:

1 cup Kalamata olives, pitted*

1 Tbsp olive oil

2 tsp fresh garlic, minced

1 tsp fresh rosemary

1 pinch sea salt

 **Chef's Serving Suggestions**

- These are high in sodium, but stick to the serving size and they can be a tasty addition to a party.
- The flavor will be smoother the longer they marinate.
- Use black olives instead of Kalamata olives.
- Slice up and add to salads, wraps and sandwiches. Watch your portion size! Stick with two!

1 Mix together and allow to marinade—the longer the better.

2 Serve in a dish with toothpicks.

*Contact manufacturer to ensure product is gluten-free.*

1 Blend all ingredients together in food processor or small blender.

*Contact manufacturer to ensure product is gluten-free.*

 **Chef's Serving Suggestions**

- This blend is perfect to use as a stuffing or crust for beef tenderloin or chicken breast.
- You could also spread a thin layer of this on 100% sprouted whole grain bread.

# Navy Bean Puree

Makes 3 cups • Serving size: ½ cup
Total time: 1 hour 15 minutes (largely unattended)
or see quick prep (10 minutes) below

##  What you'll need:

1 tsp olive oil

¼ cup onions, chopped

1 clove garlic, minced

4 cups low-sodium chicken stock* or water

2 whole bay leaves

½ tsp fresh thyme

½ tsp fresh rosemary, chopped

3 cups navy beans *(pre-soaked for 8 hours)*

1. Heat the olive oil in a sauce pot over medium heat.

*Contact manufacturer to ensure product is gluten-free.*

2. Add the onions and garlic. Sauté for 2–3 minutes or until the onions and garlic begin to brown.

3. Add low-sodium chicken stock, bay leaves, and thyme.

4. Simmer for 10 minutes and then add drained navy beans.

5. Cook at a simmer for 50–60 minutes or until the beans are soft, but not falling apart.

6. Drain the water from the beans and place the hot beans in a food processor.

7. Add the fresh rosemary and blend until combined.

###  Chef's Serving Suggestions

- To make this a quick fix, use 3 cans of low-sodium navy beans.* Heat to a boil, then drain. Blend hot beans with thyme, rosemary, onions and garlic.

- Use this bean puree to:
  *Thicken soups*

  *Spread on 100% whole grain tortillas for nutritious wraps.*

  *Use in place of refried beans for taco night.*

  *Serve as a dip with 100% stone ground tortilla chips, 100% whole grain pita chips or raw vegetables.*

  *Use as a spread on 100% whole grain crackers and top with fresh pico de gallo (see Pico de Gallo recipe) as a quick appetizer.*

  *Also great as a side dish!*

# Stuffed Portobello Mushrooms

Makes 4 servings • Serving size: ½ stuffed mushroom • Prep time: 15 minutes
Cook time: 1 hour (unattended)

 **What you'll need:**

1 pound button mushrooms *(clean and remove stems)*

2 tsp fresh garlic, minced *(or 2 cloves)*

1 tsp fresh thyme

¼ tsp sea salt

2 Portobello mushroom caps *(cleaned)*

5 Tbsp Ezekiel bread crumbs *(made from 1 slice whole grain Ezekiel bread)* Ezekiel bread crumbs can be substituted with gluten-free oat bran

Olive oil or spray

1. Preheat oven to 350° and line a broiler pan with parchment paper or lightly coat with olive oil or cooking spray.

2. Combine button mushrooms, garlic, thyme, and salt in a blender or food processor. Blend until well combined.

3. Divide stuffing mix in half and fill each Portobello mushroom cap with half the stuffing mix.

4. Sprinkle 2½ Tbsp bread crumbs on top of the stuffing mix on each mushroom.

5. Bake for 1 hour.

6. Remove from oven and allow to cool for 5 minutes before cutting in half and serving.

 **Chef's Serving Suggestions**

- These stuffed mushrooms are great served with ¼ cup marinara sauce (see recipe for *Marinara Sauce*) drizzled over top, or spread marinara in a shallow dish and place mushrooms on top of the sauce.

- This is a great appetizer or side dish.

- You can cut these "big guys" into quarters and serve on small dishes as a hors d' oeuvre.

- Serve with baked organic chicken and an organic green salad for a complete meal.

- You can also prepare them along with baked salmon. Serve them with the *Caper Tomato Sauce* recipe and some steamed veggies for a *Healthy Edge* approved feast.

- 100% whole grain crackers can be substituted for bread crumbs. Crush in a food processor.

## THE LEGACY OF A MOM

**AS I CAME INTO THE KITCHEN I NOTICED MY SON SNEAKING BROWN SUGAR OUT OF THE CONTAINER.** I became sick to my stomach as reality hit me. I thought that I could hide my addiction from my kids but they were becoming me—the part I didn't want

them to become. I began to realize that if I did not get off the roller coaster of cravings that serious illness would hit. I was only 39 and I was having symptoms of things I was afraid to go to the doctor for. I thought I knew how to change, but the desire to do it never outweighed the instant gratification that I got from food. I needed more sugar to get the same "energy" and it scared me. I actually thought about what life would be like for my family if I died. I realized how selfish I was. I couldn't believe I desired the quick fix rather than my long term health.

**BEFORE**

I began *The Healthy Edge* lifestyle and my family immediately noticed. I was kinder, happier, and spent more time with them. I released 30 pounds and dropped 4 dress sizes. We began to go on walks together, play at the park and laugh more. My lifestyle change started to affect how they ate and how active they were. As a family, we began doing 5K races.

*The Healthy Edge* has showed me the mental part of what had been going on inside me. Because of that journey on the inside the changes are life-long for me. I can't believe my kids actually ask what is better for them when they are deciding what to eat. They ask about the ingredients of foods. They take their vitamins faithfully.

Since completing *The Healthy Edge* lifestyle program, we have added two foster kids to our large family. They have been exposed to how and why to eat healthily, something they have never experienced before.

Physically, their pooch bellies are disappearing! Emotionally, they are not bouncing off the walls. They are learning life skills that are invaluable.

**AFTER**

Our oldest daughter chooses not to eat at McDonalds anymore. My son loves all the food we get to eat! The kids are excited about the new recipes and love them. One day the kids were given some boxed "mac and cheese." I let them eat it for one meal and then was going to throw out the rest. They were really excited to eat the stuff... until they started eating it. After being on *The Healthy Edge* food, the box food actually tasted like eating the box. They

didn't finish their food! My daughter, who can't have dairy, had a Healthy Edge meal instead of the "mac and cheese." She told me she got the better deal! Now the processed box stuff is not exciting to them. I can't believe the changes in our lives!

*The Healthy Edge* dives into so many personal growth components. We have fun asking "what 'R' was that?" which is a concept in *The Healthy Edge* program we really identified with. We have made some cues to help the whole family stay in 'responsible' instead of 'victim' mode. These are lifelong gifts we have given to ourselves and our family. Thank you, Healthy Edge, for influencing our family!

## Tamara Horton, USA
**RELEASED 30 POUNDS AND DROPPED 4 SIZES**

# Baked Cauliflower

Makes 4 servings • Serving size: 1 cup
Prep time: 5 minutes • Cook time: 1 hour

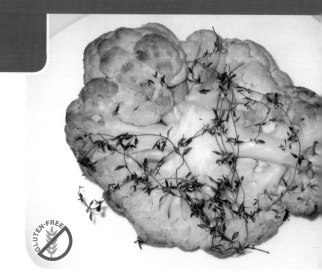

 **What you'll need:**

½ head cauliflower

1½ Tbsp olive oil

2 tsp fresh thyme *(1 tsp dried)*

½ tsp fresh rosemary, chopped
 *(¼ tsp dried)*

Pinch of sea salt

2 cloves fresh garlic, chopped or minced

1. Preheat oven to 350°.

2. Toss all ingredients, except cauliflower, together in a small bowl.

3. Pour mixture onto a sheet of aluminum foil. You need enough aluminum foil to be able to wrap up the cauliflower.

4. Place cauliflower (as pictured above) on the aluminum foil and on top of the marinade.

5. Close foil and fold to secure.

6. Bake 45 minutes to 1 hour.

 **Chef's Serving Suggestions**

- Cook time will vary depending on size of the cauliflower head.

- Cauliflower is cooked thoroughly when tender. Insert a knife to the center and if goes through easily, it is ready.

- If you double this recipe, cut the cauliflower head in half. Cook time will be much longer if cooking a whole head.

- Serve with any of the pork recipes or *Not Your Mom's Meatloaf* recipe.

# Grilled Asparagus

Makes 2 servings • Serving size: 1 cup
Prep time: 5 minutes • Cook time 5–8 minutes

# Pearl Barley & Edamame

Makes 4 servings • Serving size: 1 cup
Cook time: 1 hour (largely unattended)

 **What you'll need:**

3½ cups low-sodium chicken stock

1 cup pearled barley

¾ cup frozen edamame *(shelled)*

¾ cup mushrooms, quartered

 **Chef's Serving Suggestions**

- Add ¾ cup diced cooked organic turkey or chicken breast to turn this side into a main dish.

- Serve 1 cup over ½ cup chopped organic spinach.

- Add ¾ cup black beans at the same time as edamame for a slight variation.

- The stock reduces as it simmers. The dish could be too salty if you add any salt during the cooking process. Add salt to taste after serving. Chances are you won't need any.

❶ Combine chicken stock and barley in a pot. Bring to a low boil, then reduce heat and simmer 40 minutes.

❷ Add edamame and mushrooms. Cook on low heat for 20 additional minutes.

 **What you'll need:**

1 pound green asparagus

2 Tbsp olive oil

¼ tsp sea salt

❶ Cut ½ inch off blunt ends of asparagus.

❷ Toss all ingredients together.

❸ Grill 5–8 minutes.

# Baked Eggplant

Makes 4–6 servings
Prep time: 5 minutes
Cook time: 45 minutes

 **What you'll need:**

1 eggplant *(approximately 8" in length)*

3 tsp olive oil *(separated)*

1 clove fresh garlic, minced

2 sprigs fresh rosemary

2 sprigs fresh thyme

4 Tbsp freshly grated organic Parmesan cheese*

4 tsp olive oil

**EGGPLANT BEFORE & DURING COOKING**

1. Preheat oven to 350° and prepare a broiler pan with olive oil or spray.

2. Trim off top of eggplant (at the stem) and cut in half.

3. Brush ½ tsp olive oil onto each open side of the eggplant.

4. Sprinkle minced garlic over eggplant, equally onto each open side, and then sprinkle Parmesan cheese.

5. Place one sprig each of rosemary and thyme on each half of the eggplant. This will be on top of the cheese.

6. Heat 2 tsp olive oil in 12" pan over medium-high heat until oil just begins to ripple.

7. Sear eggplant (open side down with herb sprigs) in pan for about 2 minutes or until golden brown and transfer to broiler pan.

8. Bake 45 minutes.

*Contact manufacturer to ensure product is gluten-free.*

 **Chef's Serving Suggestions**

- Serve with roasted chicken, *Mediterranean Zucchini*, and/or *Baked Cauliflower* recipes.

- For added flavor, add the *Marinara Sauce* or the *Tomato Caper Sauce* on top of the eggplant.

# Spaghetti Squash

Makes about 5 servings
Serving size: 1 cup • Prep time: 10 minutes
Cook time: 2 hours 30 minutes (unattended)

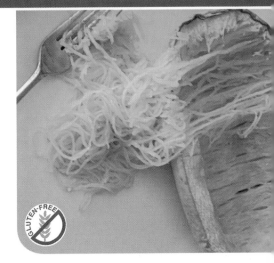

## What you'll need:

1 large spaghetti squash
2 tsp olive oil, divided
10 sprigs fresh thyme
¼ tsp sea salt, divided
2 tsp olive oil

1. Preheat oven to 300°.

2. Cut spaghetti squash in half lengthwise.  Scoop out seeds and discard.

3. Brush or rub 1 tsp olive oil onto each open side of squash.

4. Put 5 sprigs of thyme on each side of squash.

5. Sprinkle 1/8 tsp (1 pinch) of salt on each squash.

6. Place squash on broiler pan open side up, uncovered. (Broiler pan allows for air circulation underneath.  Squash cooked on cookie sheet or pan may burn on the bottom).

7. Bake for 2 to 2½ hours.

8. After squash is cooked and soft to the touch, dig out squash with a fork and it will shred like spaghetti noodles.

## Chef's Serving Suggestions

- The squash will keep in the refrigerator for up to 5 days.
- Serve with marinara sauce (see *Marinara Sauce* recipe).
- Use in the *Spaghetti Squash Salad* recipe or in the *Spaghetti Squash* and *Chicken Casserole* recipe.  Enjoy!

# Mediterranean Zucchini

Makes 4 servings
Serving size: 1 cup each
Total prep time: 10 minutes

##  What you'll need:

1½ tsp olive oil

1 zucchini squash, roughly chopped

1 yellow squash, roughly chopped

½ sweet onion, chopped

3 cloves garlic, chopped

1 tsp fresh thyme *(½ tsp dried)*

1 tsp fresh rosemary *(½ tsp dried)*

1 cup organic cherry or Roma tomatoes, chopped

½ tsp sea salt

1 sprinkle fresh ground black pepper

❶ In a medium pan on medium-high heat, add olive oil and heat for 30 seconds.

❷ Add zucchini and sauté for 2 minutes.

❸ Add onions, garlic, thyme, and rosemary and sauté for 3 minutes.

❹ Add tomatoes, salt, and pepper. Cook for 1 minute then remove from pan and serve.

## 👨‍🍳 Chef's Serving Suggestions

• Increase the serving size to 2 cups each and serve with 6 oz. of organic lean meat and 1/2 cup fresh fruit for a complete meal.

# Asparagus & Tomato Half-Casserole

Makes 2 Servings
Prep time: 10 minutes
Cook time: 30 minutes

 **What you'll need:**

1 pound asparagus *(washed and ends trimmed)*

1 tsp olive oil *(plus a bit more for inside baking dish)*

4 organic Roma tomatoes, diced

¼ tsp sea salt

1 cup low-fat organic Ricotta cheese*

Olive oil or coconut oil

1. Preheat oven to 350°. Lightly coat inside of a 7"x 9" small casserole dish with olive oil or coconut oil.

2. Mix asparagus and olive oil. Place in the baking dish.

3. Cover with tomatoes, sprinkle salt and top with Ricotta cheese.

4. Cover with aluminum foil and bake 30 minutes.

   *Contact manufacturer to ensure product is gluten-free.*

 **Chef's Serving Suggestions**

- Serve with the *Sunday Baked Chicken* or *Oat Crusted Chicken Breast* recipe.
- For a complete meal, double the recipe and add 8–10 oz. cubed or shredded pre-cooked organic chicken or turkey.

# Grilled Cauliflower & Hearts of Palm

Makes 4 servings
Serving size: 1 cup
Total prep time: 15 minutes

 ## What you'll need:

½ head cauliflower *(pre-blanched for 30–40 seconds, see below)*

1 can low-sodium hearts of palm* *(drained and cut into bite-size pieces)*

½ cup black beans*

½ tsp sea salt

2 organic Roma tomatoes, diced

1/3 cup raw, unsalted pine nuts

1 tsp olive oil

Fresh chives, chopped *(optional)*

① Cut and wash the cauliflower. Place in boiling water for 30–40 seconds.

② Drain water and combine with all other ingredients.

③ Turn out onto aluminum foil and fold over to close foil.

④ Place on hot grill for about 10 minutes.

⑤ Sprinkle with chives. (optional)

*Contact manufacturer to ensure product is gluten-free.*

**HEARTS OF PALM** are vegetables harvested from the inner core of certain palm trees. It is typically enjoyed in salads or as a vegetable side dish.

 ### Chef's Serving Suggestions

• You can cook in the oven at 350° for 25 minutes.

# Lentils with Edamame

Makes 5 cups
Serving size: 1 cup
Total time: 45 minutes

## What you'll need:

3 cups low-sodium chicken or vegetable stock*

2 tsp olive oil

1 cup lentils *(dry)*

1 onion, diced

1 clove garlic, minced

1 tsp fresh thyme *(½ tsp dried)*

1 cup shelled edamame *(frozen)*

2 Tbsp raw, unsalted pine nuts

1 organic yellow bell pepper, chopped

2 organic Roma tomatoes, diced

5 oz. crumbled organic feta cheese* *(optional)*

1. Heat olive oil in sauce pan on medium-high heat for 45 seconds.

2. Add onions and garlic. Sauté for 1 minute.

3. Add stock, lentils, and thyme.

4. Bring to a boil, reduce heat. Simmer for 30 minutes.

5. Stir in edamame, pine nuts, peppers, and tomatoes. Simmer for additional 15 minutes.

6. Remove from heat and serve.

7. Top each serving with 1 oz. crumbled organic feta cheese if desired.

*Contact manufacturer to ensure product is gluten-free.*

**LENTILS** have been part of the human diet since the Neolithic times. With 26% protein, lentils have the third highest level of protein from any plant based food after soybeans and hemp. From a nutrient perspective, lentils are high in dietary fiber and an excellent source of iron and muscle building protein.

### Chef's Serving Suggestions

- You can double the serving size and prepare recipe as a meal for lunch or dinner.

- Double the recipe and prepare in a crock pot. Just add all ingredients together (except peppers and feta) and cook on high heat for about 2 hours. Add the peppers 20 minutes before end of cook time. Sprinkle each serving with organic feta cheese.

# Easy Lentils & Edamame with Avocado

Makes 4 servings • Serving size: 1 cup each
Prep time: under 5 minutes
Cook time: 35 minutes, largely unattended

 **What you'll need:**

2 cups low-sodium chicken stock*

1 cup dried lentils

1 cup frozen edamame

2 organic Roma tomatoes, cubed

2 Tbsp red onion, diced

1 tsp fresh thyme

1 tsp sea salt

1 avocado, cubed

1 Place all ingredients together in a sauce pot, except avocado.

2 Bring to a boil, cover, reduce heat and simmer on medium-low for 30 minutes.

3 Remove from heat, stir gently, and transfer to a serving dish.

4 Gently stir in the cubed avocado. Over-stirring will make the avocado turn to mush.

*Contact manufacturer to ensure product is gluten-free.

**EDAMAME** are young, green soybeans often sold in the pod. Edamame are high in protein as well as dietary fiber, iron and calcium. They are low in saturated fat, cholesterol-free, and a source of omega-3 fatty acids.

 **Chef's Serving Suggestions**

• Easily turn this veggie side dish into a quick meal by adding pre-cooked, diced:
  *Organic pork loin*
  *Organic chicken or turkey breast*
  *Organic grass-fed beef tenderloin*

# Brown Basmati Rice with Summer Vegetables

Makes 6 servings (as a side), 3 servings (as a meal)
Serving size: 1 cup (as a side), 2 cups (as a meal)
Prep time: 10 minutes • Cook time: 25 minutes

 **What you'll need:**

1½ cups pre-cooked quinoa pasta

3 Tbsp red onion, diced

2/3 cup black beans*

1 cup pre-cooked brown basmati rice

2 Tbsp olive oil

1 cup organic baby spinach, chopped

1 cup zucchini, chopped

1 cup yellow squash, chopped

2 cups Portobello mushrooms, chopped

3 organic Roma tomatoes, diced in chunks

1 Preheat oven to 350°.

2 Mix all ingredients together in a bowl.

3 Transfer to baking dish and cover with foil.

4 Bake for 25 minutes or until squash is tender.

*Contact manufacturer to ensure product is gluten-free.*

**QUINOA** (pronounced KEEN-WAH) flour is used in various pastas, breads, pancake mixes, etc. The flour contains no gluten. Quinoa was referred to as the "Mother Grain" in the Inca culture. They considered it a wonder food, just as today it is billed as a super grain because it is high in protein, fiber and many vitamins and minerals. When preparing quinoa, the small seeds should be washed thoroughly before cooking to remove the bitter coating called saponin.

 **Chef's Serving Suggestions**

• You can replace the quinoa pasta with 1½ cups brown basmati rice.
• For extra flavor add 1 tsp fresh thyme and 1 large clove garlic, minced (or 1½ tsp).
• This dish is great with a light fish such as salmon, tilapia, or red snapper.

## NOT ANOTHER DIET!

**I STARTED THE HEALTHY EDGE IN JUNE OF 2009 UNDER DURESS.** My wife, Lauris, had told me while on vacation that she wanted us to start this new way of eating when we returned home. I immediately thought, "Not another diet." What a diet usually means for me is losing 10 to 20 pounds, and then finding 25 or 30 pounds later. As a good husband does, I always try to support my wife, so I agreed to give it a try when we got home.

**BEFORE**

We did the recommended Jump Start program the first week. I ate every 2½ to 3 hours, drank water, and wasn't hungry. After the first week, the cravings were gone and I had released 11 pounds. After two or three weeks I noticed that I was now going up the two flights of stairs at my place of work two stairs at a time. When I reached the top, I was not out of breath and felt better than I had in a very long time.

Sixteen weeks into eating more healthy and taking a pharmaceutical grade supplement, I had released 40 pounds and felt better than I had in 20 years. After 24 weeks I have released about 47 pounds. I have gone from a size 46 waist back to a size 38. My neck went from 18½ inches to 16½ inches. I didn't know people lost weight in their neck!

*The Healthy Edge* gave me the tools and mindset to be able to release the weight that I never thought I would without a strict and miserable diet. I have hardly exercised during this journey, so I think that if I add some sort of exercise I will continue to release even more weight. However, this is not just about losing the weight for me; it is about me living a healthier and more fulfilling life today and for the future.

I thank Amber and April for sharing their story and giving me and many others the opportunity to learn a new, healthier way of living.

**AFTER**

## ART BYRD, USA
**RELEASED 47 POUNDS IN 24 WEEKS**

# SALADS

AFTER

**WHEN WE FIRST STARTED THE HEALTHY EDGE, WE WERE A LITTLE SKEPTICAL ABOUT THE COSTS FOR FOLLOWING THE PROGRAM AND THE CHANGES WHICH WOULD BE REQUIRED TO FOLLOW IT.** After 8 weeks, we did some comparisons on the costs and were pleasantly surprised. We had a savings of $327.61 in our first month of *The Healthy Edge* program. This was quite a substantial drop considering we were now purchasing some organic foods and pharmaceutical grade nutritional supplements. The first month's savings more than covered the small cost of getting the opportunity to become healthy and change our lives with *The Healthy Edge*.

Our lifestyle has been transformed by what we learned in *The Healthy Edge* program. It has re-oriented us both physically and emotionally. It's not only about "what" we eat but also about "why" we eat. This new lifestyle has impacted the health of our family and friends. In six months, I have released 27 lbs. I began in a size 14 and I am now wearing a size 6. I love the way I look and feel! But more important than the weight release is how EASY it has been. Since we eat every few hours, we are never hungry. We don't count calories or points and we have energy throughout the day, we sleep all night and are FREE from cravings! You can do it too!

AFTER

**LAURIS BYRD, USA**
**RELEASED 26 POUNDS AND WENT
FROM A SIZE 14 TO A SIZE 6**

# Cucumber & Tomato Salad

Makes 4 cups
Serving size: 1 cup (as side) or 2 cups (as salad)
Total prep time: 5–10 minutes

 **What you'll need:**

1 English *(seedless)* cucumber

2 organic Roma tomatoes, cubed

1 medium red onion, chopped

2 Tbsp Balsamic vinegar*

2 Tbsp extra virgin olive oil

 **1** Mix all ingredients together and serve immediately or chill for up to 6 hours.

*Contact manufacturer to ensure product is gluten-free.*

 **Chef's Serving Suggestions**

- The salad has the best flavor when the oil and vinegar marinate for about an hour. It will get slightly mushy if it marinates more than 6–8 hours before serving.

- Prepare up to a day or two ahead of time and add the oil and vinegar an hour before serving.

- You can also drizzle the oil and vinegar as needed! That's *The Healthy Edge* way!

- Dress it up with chives or ½ cup organic feta cheese.*

- No salt needed, try it and love it without!

# Black Bean Salad

Makes 4 servings (total 2 cups)
Serving size: ½ cup
Prep time: 6–10 minutes

 **What you'll need:**

1 organic Roma tomato, diced

1 cup black beans* *(canned or pre-cooked)*

½ cup whole kernel corn* *(canned or pre-cooked)*

2 Tbsp red onion, diced

1 tsp olive oil

½ tsp sea salt

Garnish with broccoli or alfalfa sprouts
*(optional)*

 **①** Mix all ingredients together.

*Contact manufacturer to ensure product is gluten-free.*

 **Chef's Serving Suggestions**

- This salad is also tasty topped with 2–3 oz. crumbled organic feta cheese.*
- Make it the night before and have ready to pack for your lunch or the kids.
- Serve with some home-baked tortilla chips as a hors d' oeuvre.

# Broccoli and Pomegranate Salad

Makes approximately 4 servings
Serving size: 3/4 cup each
Cook and prep time under 30 minutes

 **What you'll need:**

5 cups water
3½ cups fresh broccoli
1 Tbsp chopped red onions
¾ cup pomegranate seeds
2 Tbsp Balsamic vinegar*
3 Tbsp olive oil
1 tsp sea salt
¼ cup raw, unsalted pine nuts*

1. In a medium pot, bring water to a boil.

2. Add broccoli and boil for 3 minutes.

3. Drain and rinse broccoli with cold water to stop the cooking process. This will prevent it from continuing to cook and becoming mushy.

4. In a separate bowl, combine remaining ingredients to make pomegranate dressing.

5. Toss Broccoli together with dressing and serve.

   *Contact manufacturer to ensure product is gluten-free.*

 **Chef's Serving Suggestions**

• This is best served immediately; broccoli and pine nuts will become mushy the longer it sits.
• You can also drizzle the dressing on the broccoli as needed. That's *The Healthy Edge* way!

# Chicken Salad

Makes 4 servings
Serving size: ¾ cup
Prep time: under 10 minutes

## What you'll need:

1 cup shredded cooked organic chicken

½ cup organic celery, chopped

¾ cup organic apple, chopped

2 Tbsp onions, chopped

2 Tbsp raw, unsalted pine nuts or walnuts*

½ tsp sea salt

½ cup low-fat plain organic yogurt*

½ cup organic grapes, cut in half

1 Mix all ingredients together.

*Contact manufacturer to ensure product is gluten-free.

### Chef's Serving Suggestions

- Use left over baked, boiled, or grilled chicken for this recipe.

- Serve over a bed of organic greens, with raw veggies, in a 100% whole grain pita, on 100% whole grain bread or all by itself.  So many ways to enjoy this yummy chicken salad!

- Sprinkle with some ground cayenne pepper for a little kick.

# Fruit Salad

Makes 5 cups
Serving size: 1 cup
Prep time: 10 – 15 minutes

 **What you'll need:**

2 oranges

2 bananas

1 organic apple

1 cup organic grapes

1 cup organic strawberries

½ cup organic blueberries

¼ cup sliced raw, unsalted almonds *(optional)*

1 Wash and cut all fruit into medium size chunks and mix together.

2 The oranges will keep the bananas and apples from immediately browning.

 **Chef's Serving Suggestions**

- This fruit salad is easily prepared the night before for a wonderful breakfast treat.
- Serve the fruit salad with some protein for a complete meal or snack.
- Sliced almonds will add some quality protein and healthy fat to lower the glycemic index.
- Mix ½ cup organic yogurt and 1 cup fruit salad.
- Mix ½ cup organic cottage cheese and 1 cup fruit salad.
- Serve with 3–5 cooked organic egg whites and ½ cup fruit salad.
- Serve with 1 piece of organic string cheese and ½ cup fruit salad.

# Grilled Asparagus Salad

Makes 2 servings
Serving size: 1 cup
Total prep time: 20 minutes

## What you'll need:

2 Tbsp olive oil

2 Tbsp Balsamic vinegar*

½ tsp sea salt

2 Portobello mushrooms *(whole, cleaned, and stems removed)*

1 pound green asparagus *(washed and ends trimmed about 1–1½ inch)*

¼ cup organic feta cheese, crumbled*

1. Mix together olive oil, vinegar and salt, and toss with mushrooms.

2. Place asparagus and mushrooms on grill, for about 7–10 minutes.

3. Remove from grill and cut asparagus into 1–2 inch segments and cube or thinly slice Portobello mushrooms.

4. Toss together asparagus, mushrooms, organic feta cheese, and serve immediately.

*Contact manufacturer to ensure product is gluten-free.*

### Chef's Serving Suggestions

- Asparagus should be green and crunchy. Cook times will vary depending on the type and style of your grill, so keep an eye on it! Old-fashioned charcoal grills add a smoky flavor.

- Make the most of your grill time. Throw on some extra chicken breasts to refrigerate or freeze for faster recipes during the hectic work week.

# Portobello Mushroom Salad

Makes 2 servings • Serving size: 1 cup
Prep time: 10 minutes • Marinating time: 30–60
minutes • Cook time 7–10 minutes

 **What you'll need:**

2 Portobello mushrooms *(stems removed)*

¼ cup Balsamic vinegar*

2 cloves garlic, minced

2 Tbsp olive oil

1 organic Roma tomato, diced

1 Tbsp fresh chives, chopped

1  Cut mushrooms in half or leave whole and place in a bowl.

2  Combine Balsamic vinegar, garlic, and olive oil in separate bowl.

3  Pour mixture over mushrooms.  Stir well to completely coat mushrooms.

4  Marinate 30–60 minutes.

5  Grill mushrooms 7–10 minutes.

6  Cut up mushrooms.

7  Add tomatoes and chives.  Stir and serve.

*Contact manufacturer to ensure product is gluten-free.*

# Shrimp Salad with Avocado

Makes 4 appetizer servings
Cook and prep time: under 30 minutes

## What you'll need:

5 cups water

1 tsp sea salt

2 dried bay leaves

10 whole juniper berries*

20 raw frozen 31/40 size shrimp**

1 tsp sweet onions, chopped

½ tsp olive oil

¼ tsp sea salt

½ tsp fresh garlic, chopped or minced

½ tsp fresh dill, chopped

2 avocados, peeled and pit removed

1. In a medium stock pot, combine water, salt, bay leaves, and juniper berries.

2. Bring to a boil, add shrimp.

3. Boil for 4 minutes, remove shrimp and place in an ice water bath for 10 minutes. (In a bowl of ice water)

4. While shrimp is cooling, stir together remaining ingredients, except avocado.

5. Peel and de-vein shrimp. Stir them into the dill mixture.

*JUNIPER BERRIES are a pine flavored dried berry. They can be found in your local grocery store or easily located in a health food store. They can also be found at your local farmer's market.

** SHRIMP are generally sold according to how many come per pound. If purchasing fresh or frozen shrimp they will be labeled 16/20 or 31/40. (This means there is between 31 and 40 shrimp per pound.) If you don't see this on the package, you will need about 12 oz. of shrimp. You can use fresh shrimp for this recipe as well.

## Chef's Serving Suggestions

- To serve, place half of a sliced avocado onto a plate and add 5 coated shrimp. Garnish with one sprig of fresh dill.

- Chop shrimp and remove tails. Serve with thinly sliced avocado and fresh dill. This can be presented on small individual plates as a party appetizer.

# Spaghetti Squash Salad

Makes 4 servings
Serving size: ¾ cup
Total prep time: 10 minutes

 **What you'll need:**

1½ cup cooked spaghetti squash
*(see the Spaghetti Squash recipe)*

1 organic Roma tomato, diced

2 Tbsp fresh cilantro, chopped
*(1 Tbsp dried)*

1 Tbsp extra virgin olive oil

1 tsp white wine vinegar* or
white Balsamic vinegar*

3 Tbsp canned low-sodium black
beans* *(drained and rinsed)*

¼ tsp sea salt

 ❶ Mix all ingredients together.

*Contact manufacturer to ensure product is gluten-free.*

 **Chef's Serving Suggestions**

- Top with some crumbled organic feta cheese* for even more zest!
- Dried black beans are the healthiest option. Follow instructions on the bag. Making black beans in bulk can allow you to use in additional recipes.

# Warm Chicken Salad

Makes 2 servings • Serving size: 1½ cup each
Prepared in under 10 minutes if using
pre-cooked chicken

## What you'll need:

1 cup edamame, frozen

1 cup whole corn kernels, frozen

2 tsp red onions, minced

1 cup pre-cooked organic chicken, cubed or shredded

1 tsp stone ground mustard*

1 tsp olive oil

1 pinch of sea salt

1. Heat oil in sauté pan over medium-high heat.

2. Combine edamame, corn, and onions and sauté for 2 minutes.

3. Add chicken and mustard. Continue to sauté until chicken is warm throughout.

4. Stir in salt.

5. Serve alone, over a bed of greens, or in a 100% whole grain pita or tortilla.

   *Contact manufacturer to ensure product is gluten-free.

**WHOLE GRAIN MUSTARD** is a type of mustard produced when the mustard seeds (white, brown, black) are not ground up, but mixed with other ingredients. Substitute Dijon mustard. Be sure to read the ingredient list.

### Chef's Serving Suggestions

- Use fresh or pre-cooked edamame or corn.

- You can also bring 4 cups water to boil in a pot over high heat. Add edamame and corn, cook 3–4 minutes, drain water, and then proceed to sauté with chicken.

- Great to use left over baked, boiled, or grilled chicken for this, but if you are starting with raw chicken, sauté cubed chicken 3–4 minutes prior to adding the edamame and corn.

# BREAKING THE CYCLE

**I CAN'T REMEMBER THE FIRST TIME A BOY KISSED ME, BUT I CAN REMEMBER THE FIRST TIME A BOY CALLED ME A "GROSS PIG."** I can't remember if I was in first or second grade, but I can vividly remember the shame that ran through me. My childhood is sprinkled with these stories, equally painful and equally humiliating.

As I grew older, the only thing that changed was the crudity of the comments. The shame burned into me and I began to tell myself the same things: I never had seconds; I "pigged out." I never treated myself to birthday cake; I ate "badly." And no matter how hard I tried or wished or prayed, I repeated this over and over.

**BEFORE**

For me, sugar is an addiction. The emotional turmoil, the heartbreak and desperation it has caused me is boundless. The treatments or "diets" have been disappointing failures. No matter what I did, I would always find myself back at the table wondering what happened.

By 49 years old I had pretty much given up. I wanted something sweet every night, and I had it. And, except for my nightly binges, I thought I ate good food. Organic, no preservatives, minimal processing, nothing fried, no fast food, everything whole grains (except cookies, cakes, doughnuts, etc.). I rationalized my morning pot of coffee and 4 or 5 diet Mountain Dews every day.

I was tired. I didn't sleep well. I didn't connect my irritability and depression to the food I ate. I blamed my family, my mom, the school system; everything but what I was choosing to eat.

**AFTER**

Deep inside I knew there was a better way to live, but I had run out of ideas to find it. But just after my birthday, I listened to a motivational speaker, Amber Thiel, and a bit of hope came back. I am not really sure what power directed me to her lecture that day but it was a tipping point in my life.

*The Healthy Edge* is not a quick-fix-get-skinny program, but a program based in science and facts. This program addressed not just the physical but the emotional aspects of eating. I watched the very first video and I was so relieved, I felt tearful. I knew a lot about physiology of the human body but I had never heard of the concept of "Insulin Resistance."

I realized that there was nothing wrong with my head. I wasn't an "out of control pig." My body was simply out of balance, and *The Healthy Edge* offered me a way to balance it and keep it that way.

I followed the program 100%. Within 5 DAYS THE CRAVINGS WERE GONE! A lifetime of struggling and... poof! I had freedom from sugar binges.

How is my life different today? My life is no longer controlled by food. I choose what I eat. My food does not choose me. And months later, I am still craving-free. This is one of the most profound experiences of my life. I sleep peacefully and restfully each night. My moods are stable and my depression is gone. I eat a lot and often so I have energy. I've released over 16 pounds and 4% body fat just during the seven weeks of *The Healthy Edge* program. I'm wearing peg-legged, low-cut jeans and I couldn't be more proud. My life is excellent, exactly as it should be.

**AFTER**

## JAN HICKLING, USA
**RELEASED 16 POUNDS IN 7 WEEKS**

# Pita Florentine

Makes 2 servings • Prep time: 5-10 minutes
Cook time: 8 minutes

 **What you'll need:**

- 1 100% whole or sprouted grain pita
- 2½ cups organic baby spinach, chopped
- 1 tsp fresh garlic, chopped
- 1 Tbsp red onion, chopped
- 2 organic egg whites pre-cooked *(boiled eggs)*
- 1 organic Roma tomato, diced
- ¼ tsp sea salt
- ½ cup cubed or crumbled organic feta cheese

**PITA** pictured with *Pearl Barley and Edamame*

1. Pre-heat oven to 300°.

2. Mix all ingredients together.

3. Cut pita in half.

4. Stuff each half of pita with ½ cup of mixture.

5. Bake in folded aluminum foil on a broiler pan for 8 minutes. (Pita should be covered with the foil but don't seal the edges.)

# Pita Sandwich

Makes 1 serving
Prep time: 10 minutes

 **What you'll need:**

1 100% whole or sprouted grain pita

½ cup organic baby spinach, chopped

½ organic Roma tomato, diced

¼ tsp olive oil

½ oz. *(2 Tbsp)* fresh *(curd) organic*
   mozzarella or vegan mozzarella
   *(sliced)*

1 Tbsp organic feta cheese, crumbled
   or cubed

❶ Turn on sandwich maker or indoor electric grill.

❷ Slice off a small section on one side of the pita to create an opening to fill the pita.

❸ Mix all ingredients together and gently stuff inside the pita.

❹ Place pita in sandwich maker or grill, lower top, and cook for 3 to 4 minutes.

 **Chef's Serving Suggestions**

- Top this with fresh salsa and/or add black beans for extra fiber and protein.
- Serve with ½ cup low fat organic cottage cheese for a YUMMY lunch!
- You can also make this in an oven on a broiler pan or baking sheet at 400° for 5–7 minutes.
- Serve with a *Healthy Edge* salad, side dish, or soup for a complete meal.

# Stuffed Pita Pockets

Makes 2 stuffed pitas
Serving size: 1 stuffed pita
Total prep time: 20 minutes

## What you'll need:

⅓ cup organic Roma tomatoes, diced

⅓ cup organic baby spinach, chopped

⅓ cup fresh bean sprouts, chopped

¼ tsp olive oil

½ cup pre-cooked organic turkey or
  organic chicken breast, diced

¼ tsp sea salt

2 Tbsp black beans *(pre-cooked or use low-sodium
  canned beans, drained and rinsed)*

2 100% whole or sprouted grain pita pockets

① Heat sandwich maker or electric indoor grill.

② Cut pitas to allow opening for stuffing.

③ Mix all other ingredients together.

④ Divide mixture in half and fill pitas.

⑤ Place in sandwich maker for about 8–10 minutes.

# Pizza Pita

Makes 1 serving
Prep time: under 10 minutes

## What you'll need:

2 Tbsp marinara sauce *(see Marinara Sauce recipe)*

2 mushrooms, sliced

1 oz. *(4 Tbsp)* fresh *(curd)* organic mozzarella or vegan mozzarella *(sliced)*

½ 100% whole or sprouted grain pita

1. Heat sandwich maker or electric indoor grill.

2. Layer sauce, mushrooms, then mozzarella inside ½ pita.

3. Place pizza pita inside grill for 4–5 minutes.

## Chef's Serving Suggestions

- Stuff with other veggies like organic red bell peppers, chopped organic spinach, onions, or artichoke hearts.
- Make this in an oven on a broiler pan or baking sheet at 400° for 5–7 minutes.
- Serve with a *Healthy Edge* salad, side, or soup for a complete meal.

# Egg & Veggie Pita Pockets

Makes 2 servings
Serving size: 1/2 pita
Prep time: 10 minutes

 ## What you'll need:

½ cup organic arugula or spinach, chopped

½ cup bean sprouts, chopped

½ cup organic Roma tomatoes, diced

⅓ cup low-sodium black-eyed peas *(drained and rinsed)*

¼ cup mushrooms, chopped

2 Tbsp red onion, diced

⅓ cup organic red bell pepper, diced

3 organic egg whites, pre-cooked *(boiled eggs)*

¼ tsp sea salt

¼ tsp olive oil *(optional)*

1. Mix all ingredients together.

2. Turn on sandwich maker or indoor grill.

3. Cut pitas to allow opening for stuffing.

4. Divide mixture in half and fill pitas.

5. Cut pitas to allow opening for stuffing.

6. Place in sandwich maker for about 8–10 minutes.

 ### Chef's Serving Suggestions

- Be creative and use what you have available. When you are mixing healthy foods from your fridge, you can create different flavors and themes.

- Try stuffing in some diced or julienne sliced organic red bell peppers, organic feta cheese, thinly sliced onions, any type of bean, or some avocado… the possibilities are endless.

# Open Face Chicken Sandwich

Makes 2 servings
Serving size: 1 open face sandwich
Total time: 10–12 minutes

## What you'll need:

2 slices sprouted whole grain bread *(or 100% whole wheat bread)*

1 avocado *(cut in half, pit removed)*

½ cup organic baby spinach

1 organic Roma tomato, sliced

6 oz. pre-cooked organic chicken

4 oz. vegan mozzarella cheese for dairy free *(or fresh organic mozzarella)*

**SPROUTED GRAIN BREAD**, often referred to as Ezekiel bread, is inspired by the Holy Scripture verse Ezekiel 4:9: "Take thou also unto thee wheat, and barley, and beans, and lentils, and millet, and vetches, and put them in one vessel, and make thee bread thereof…" The sprouting process retains vital nutrients and increases vitamins found in the original grain. Sprouted grain bread is relatively high in protein and fiber.

1 Preheat oven to 375°.

2 Lightly toast bread in the toaster.

3 Spread ¼–½ avocado on each slice of bread.

4 Cover the avocado with ¼ cup spinach.

5 Top the spinach with ½ sliced tomato.

6 Layer with 3 oz. sliced pre-cooked chicken.

7 Finish off with shredded or sliced mozzarella.

8 Place in the oven on a baking sheet for 5 minutes (or until cheese is well melted).

 **Chef's Serving Suggestions**

- Ezekiel bread is made from sprouted whole grains. It toasts well and is a great source of whole grains and fiber.

- "From your Heart" vegan mozzarella is what Chef Keith uses. It melts well and actually tastes like mozzarella.

- Serve this sandwich with a small salad or *Healthy Edge* leftover.

- This can be a quick lunch or double the portion and serve as a dinner the whole family will love. Faster and healthier than take out!

# LIFE OR DEATH

**BY LATE 2000 I WAS FED UP WITH BEING FAT.** Vowing to get back into the condition I was in when I was in the military, I set out on a physical training program with the assistance of a personal trainer. Over the next 9 months (and having spent $3,000 in personal training) I lost 70 pounds through one-hour workouts every morning and two-hour workouts every evening. I followed a very regimented and restrictive diet including fat burners and protein shakes.

I fit into sizes I hadn't worn since early college. While I was very pleased with my success, my trainer warned me that if I didn't learn to eat right, all that weight I had lost would come back. I didn't listen and within 3 years I found the 70 pounds I lost and found some more along the way. I also had just been admitted to the hospital with a potential heart attack at age 41.

I needed to lose the weight or my life would be dramatically shortened. I was also suffering from an ulcer in my esophagus, cholesterol and blood pressure levels that were unreasonably high, and blood sugar levels that were rapidly headed towards diabetes, a disease that has taken several of my family members over the years.

**BEFORE**

Over the next 4 years I tried a number of diets and workouts without success. In May of 2008 my wife dragged me to a seminar about a lifestyle program which, to me, sounded like someone trying to get into my wallet. I couldn't have been more wrong.

In five months, I released 55 pounds, my blood pressure dropped from 170/110 to 112/70 and my BMI went from 34% to 26%. I am sleeping through the night and have a cholesterol level that is well within normal. I have the energy when I get home to interact with my family without being an impossible bear. Because of *The Healthy Edge* lifestyle program, I am able to live a healthy lifestyle where I eat well, take a high quality supplement, have time with my family instead of at the gym, and still enjoy occasional treats without having an impact on my lifestyle.

Thank you, Healthy Edge, you may well have saved my life.

**AFTER 7 WEEKS**

## JOHN WANAMAKER, USA • RELEASED OVER 60 POUNDS

**BEFORE**

**AFTER**

**THIS IS THE PROGRAM THAT TRANSFORMED MY BODY AND ATTITUDE AND PROBABLY SAVED MY HUSBAND JOHN'S LIFE BY HELPING US RELEASE ALMOST 100 LBS BETWEEN THE TWO OF US.** We did it without counting calories or only eating proteins, without exercising twice a day or any other fad that is unsafe and unsustainable.

At the end of *The Healthy Edge* program, we were consistently making good decisions about what we were putting in our bodies, had dropped significant weight and several sizes. Beyond a year, we still are releasing the weight and living a healthy lifestyle. It can work for you too.

**KELLY WANAMAKER, USA • RELEASED OVER 30 POUNDS**

**MY STRUGGLE TURNED INTO LIFE-THREATENING WHEN I TURNED 45 AND STARTED SOME OF THE SYMPTOMS OF MENOPAUSE.** My name is Carolyn Porter and I've been a Women's Health Care Nurse Practitioner for 25 years. In all that time and for most of my life I've struggled with weight. I tried a particularly popular diet 8 times; I did Atkins, and numerous workshops, but never got the results I was looking for. No matter what I tried, the weight would not come off. The most concerning factors was my cholesterol and triglycerides. I have a strong family history of heart disease, hypertension and diabetes. The MD who was providing my care said, "Here, take this pill, because of your family history you will never change your lab results!" I knew my only shot was to lose the weight. But how?

**BEFORE**

Everything changed in 2009! I took on my life! *The Healthy Edge* has been the program that has supported me in releasing 30 pounds, lowering my triglycerides, raising my good cholesterol and lowering the bad. The biggest accomplishment of all is that because of my good health I don't take "the pills" anymore! My health care provider is amazed that the only medicine I do take is a low-dose blood pressure pill and good quality nutritional supplements. My personal goal for the rest of my life is to run and play with my grandchildren, practice *The Healthy Edge*, and never have to take "the pill" again!

**AFTER**

**CAROLYN PORTER, USA • RELEASED OVER 30 POUNDS**

# Low-sodium Chicken Stock

Makes 8–10 cups
Prep time: 15 minutes
Cook time: 5 hours (largely unattended)

## What you'll need:

12 cups cold water

1 whole skinless organic chicken

4 bay leaves

16 whole juniper berries

1 Tbsp sea salt

1 tsp whole black peppercorns

1 tsp dried oregano or marjoram

3 cloves fresh garlic, chopped

1 large onion, coarsely chopped

½ cup carrots, chopped *(washed and unpeeled)*

½ cup organic celery, chopped

2 sprigs fresh thyme *(or 2 tsp dried)*

**JUNIPER BERRY** is the female seed cone produced by various species of juniper trees. As a spice, it is commonly used to flavor meat dishes, game meats and season sauerkraut. Substitute equal parts crushed bay leaves and caraway seeds.

1. In a large pot add all ingredients.

2. Bring to a boil on high heat. Reduce heat and cook on a slow boil at medium to medium-low heat for 2½ hours.

3. Remove chicken from pot and place chicken in a bowl. Set aside.

4. Pour the liquid through a thin sieve or strainer to remove all chicken, vegetables, and spices.

5. Return strained liquid to pot and simmer on low heat for another 2 hours and 15 minutes.

6. When the stock is finished, you will want to cool it completely, quickly. Pour the stock into a tall stock pot or stainless steel bowl and place the bowl in a sink of ice water. This will allow the stock to cool quickly and evenly. After it is cooled completely, you will be able to skim the fat off the top and then divide into smaller air-tight containers and store.

### Chef's Serving Suggestions

- Use this chicken stock for many recipes in this cookbook!

- Pull the chicken meat off the bones. Use the boiled chicken on salads and for many other yummy recipes like the *Stuffed Pita Pockets, Warm Chicken Salad, Chicken and Pineapple Fajitas,* (see recipes) and many more.

- To make the stock without the whole chicken, you can use chicken bones and leftovers after you have made *Sunday Baked Chicken* (see recipe).

- You can store and refrigerate up to 7 days or freeze for up to 2–3 months.

# Cauliflower Soup

Makes 4 servings
Serving size: 1½ cup each
Prep time: 30 minutes (largely unattended)

## What you'll need:

2 Tbsp olive oil

½ medium red onion, diced

½ head cauliflower, washed and cut

½ cup dried green split peas

4 cups low-sodium chicken or
   vegetable stock*

2 dried bay leaves

1 tsp sea salt

1. Heat olive oil over medium-high heat in a medium stock pot.

2. Add onions, cauliflower, and split peas. Sauté for 2 minutes.

3. Add chicken or vegetable stock, bay leaves, and sea salt.

4. Bring to a boil, reduce heat to medium or medium-low and simmer for 25 minutes.

5. Remove bay leaves. Puree in a blender or food processor and serve.

*Contact manufacturer to ensure product is gluten-free.*

### Chef's Serving Suggestions

- Serve 1 cup soup over ½ cup chopped organic baby spinach & 5 organic cherry tomatoes. Top with 4–6 oz. grilled or baked wild caught salmon.

- Add cooked black beans or edamame after step 3 for additional protein and fiber.

- Serve soup topped with ⅓ cup fresh pico de gallo (see *Pico De Gallo* recipe) or diced organic tomatoes.

# French Onion Soup

Makes 6 servings • Serving size: 2 cups
Prep time: 10 minutes • Cook time: 1 hour 45
minutes (largely unattended)

## What you'll need:

3 Tbsp olive oil

3 lbs onions, thinly sliced

4 cloves fresh garlic, chopped

8 cups low-sodium chicken stock*

2 Tbsp fresh thyme *(1 Tbsp dried)*

1. In a large stock pot over medium heat, combine olive oil and onions.

2. Slightly caramelize onions and sauté together for 10–15 minutes.

3. Add garlic, stock, and thyme.

4. Bring to a boil, reduce heat and simmer uncovered for 1½ hours.

   *Contact manufacturer to ensure product is gluten-free.*

## Chef's Serving Suggestions

- French Onion Soup is traditionally served with toasted bread and Swiss cheese melted over top. This recipe is so flavorful that you won't miss the toasted cheese, but you could add a slice of 100% whole or sprouted grain bread (toasted) with a slice of low-fat organic Swiss cheese if you desired the traditional recipe.

- Serve this delicious soup alone or with an organic spinach salad for a complete meal.

- Serve this over a bed of chopped organic baby spinach with fresh organic cherry tomatoes.

# 20-Minute Mushroom Soup

Makes 6 servings
Serving size: 1½ cups
Total prep time: 20 minutes

## What you'll need:

3 tsp olive oil

3 cloves fresh garlic, chopped or pressed

¾ cup sweet onion, chopped

2 cups mushrooms, chopped

2 cups carrots, chopped

6 cups low-sodium chicken stock*

2 dried bay leaves

¾ cup pre-cooked low-sodium kidney beans *(or 1 (15 oz.) can drained and rinsed)*

¾ cup pre-cooked low-sodium black beans *(or 1 (15 oz.) can drained and rinsed)*

¾ cup frozen or fresh edamame

1 cup organic spinach, chopped

1 tsp sea salt

### Chef's Serving Suggestions

- For a thicker soup, whisk 1 cup hummus (see *Hummus* recipe) or use 1 cup cooked and pureed chick peas or navy beans.

1. Heat olive oil in a medium stock pot over med-high heat, until oil begins to ripple.

2. Add garlic, onions, and mushrooms. Sauté for 2 minutes.

3. Add carrots and sauté for an additional 2 minutes.

4. Add stock and bay leaves.

5. Just as soup begins to boil, add beans.

6. When soup begins to boil again, reduce heat to medium and cook for 10 minutes, stirring occasionally.

7. Stir in spinach and salt. Simmer for an additional 2 minutes, then serve.

*Contact manufacturer to ensure product is gluten-free.*

# Asian Tofu Soup

Makes 4 servings • Serving size: 2 cups
Prep time: 10 minutes • Cook time: 1 hour

## What you'll need:

2 tsp sesame oil* *(or olive oil)*

4 cloves garlic, minced

⅓ cup onions, very finely sliced

4 tsp fresh ginger, very finely sliced or grated

1 cup shitake mushrooms, chopped

2 Tbsp sake*

1 tsp raw agave nectar*

3 cups low-sodium chicken or vegetable stock*

2 baby bok choy *(cut into fourths lengthwise)*

1 cup bamboo shoots

6 oz. extra firm tofu,* cubed

**TOFU** is also known as bean curd or soybean curd. Tofu is high in protein and low in fat. It can be found in several varieties based on varying moisture contents (soft or silken tofu, regular tofu, and firm or extra firm tofu).

### Chef's Serving Suggestions

• To make this dish vegan, use vegetable stock.*

1. Heat oil in a large pot over medium heat.

2. Add garlic, onions, ginger, and mushrooms and sauté for 2 minutes.

3. In a small separate bowl, mix sake and agave nectar.

4. Add sake and agave mixture, chicken or vegetable stock, and bok choy to the pot. Bring to a boil.

5. Reduce heat and simmer for 7 minutes.

6. Stir in bamboo and tofu. Wait 2 minutes and serve.

*Contact manufacturer to ensure product is gluten-free.*

# Chicken & Mushroom Soup

Makes 4 servings
Serving size: 1½–1¾ cups each
Prep time: 15 minutes • Cook time: 1 hour

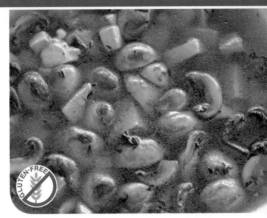

## What you'll need:

2 Tbsp olive oil

4 cups mushrooms, halved

⅓ cup fresh garlic, chopped or pressed

1 sweet onion, chopped

4 cups low-sodium chicken stock*

4 tsp fresh thyme, chopped

1 tsp sea salt

1 organic chicken breast *(cut into segments)*

1 In a medium stock pot, heat olive oil over medium-high heat and add mushrooms, garlic, and onions.

2 Sauté for 4–5 minutes.

3 Add stock, thyme, sea salt, and chicken.

4 Reduce to medium heat and simmer for 1 hour stirring occasionally.

*Contact manufacturer to ensure product is gluten-free.*

**Chef's Serving Suggestions**

• For a thicker soup, stir in 1 cup hummus (see *Hummus* recipe) or add 1 cup cooked and pureed chickpeas or navy beans.

## DIETS COSTED ME A FORTUNE

**BEFORE THE HEALTHY EDGE PROGRAM, I WAS ON THE 'ROLLERCOASTER DIET ADDICTION' WHICH, I MIGHT ADD, COSTED ME A FORTUNE!!** I would fall prey to many advertising gimmicks promising lasting success. Every time I thought to myself, "This will be the one that works!" But, every time I went off the diet I would put the weight back on plus more! This made me depressed, so I ate even more!

I had been instructed by my specialist that if I didn't lose at least 20 pounds, my medical condition—Reflux Esophagitis (caused from being overweight) would continue to get worse. I

felt very upset and carried a deep depression which I held within. I didn't understand why I had lost control over what I ate and how much! I had just pretty much given up. I was fat and that's the way I was going to stay!

I found out about *The Healthy Edge* from my very good friend, Eve. When I listened to *The Healthy Edge* program, a feeling of excitement I hadn't felt before was there. So many things that were said on the audios and DVDs made sense; I kept saying, "THAT'S HOW I FEEL, THAT'S WHAT I SAY, THAT'S JUST LIKE ME!" At last, someone understood what I was feeling and going through! That's why I chose to go on this journey.

*The Healthy Edge* is different from anything else I have tried. It is not just about losing weight; *The Healthy Edge* educated me on how, what, why, when and where.

**BEFORE**

I could write a book on how FANTASTIC this experience has been for me! *The Healthy Edge* takes you step by step through each week of the program, giving you all the tools you need to feel confident and in control. *The Healthy Edge* explained the importance of understanding and reading food labels (this was a real eye opener for me). I learned why I gained the weight and what had caused the weight to go to my belly!

**AFTER**

**BEFORE**

Some of the physical and emotional changes I experienced have been life changing. The self esteem I feel is exhilarating. I feel alive, I hold my head high and I have released 22 pounds! The reality of my amazing journey hit home when the kids took a picture of our dog and accidentally captured me also (they had always been instructed to make sure they NEVER include me in pictures), and when I saw the photo, my reaction was "Wow, I don't look like a 'fat momma anymore!" Tears are coming to my eyes as I type; the feeling was and is overwhelming! I could now sit down in jeans without being choked around my waist! In fact they are falling off me; I am able to go into the 'normal' size clothes shop and not the 'super size' shop!! My children told me how slim I look in my new clothes. Wow, that meant so much to me. These are only SOME of the changes I have experienced; there are many more!

The most powerful and dramatic effect that *The Healthy Edge* program has caused in my life is the ability to choose my food. I choose what I want to eat instead of that uncontrollable need of "I've just got to eat something, anything, and lots of it!" Those uncontrollable cravings that were leading me down the path of self destruction are gone! The physical and emotional benefits I am continuing to experience are limitless. It is a permanent eating and lifestyle change NOT a diet!

I encourage and recommend EVERYONE to do this program; not only people wanting to lose weight, but EVERYONE! The health benefits gained will give you and your family a long, healthy and happy life together as it is doing for us.

**AFTER**

**SANDI FRASER, AUSTRALIA**
**RELEASED 22 POUNDS**

# Strawberry Vinaigrette Salad Dressing

Makes ¾ cup dressing
Serving size: 2 Tbsp
Total prep time: 5 minutes

 **What you'll need:**

1 cup organic strawberries *(thawed or fresh)*

2 Tbsp white wine vinegar* or white Balsamic vinegar*

½ tsp raw agave nectar*

Pinch of sea salt *(optional)*

⅓ cup cold pressed extra virgin olive oil

❶ Blend strawberries, vinegar, agave, and salt in a blender for 10 seconds.

❷ Slowly add olive oil to mixture while blending on low. This helps to emulsify (combine) the mixture.

*\*Contact manufacturer to ensure product is gluten-free.*

 **Chef's Serving Suggestions**

- If vinaigrette does not emulsify (or if it separates) shake or stir well before use.
- Store in airtight container in refrigerator up to 5 days.
- Try this dressing on an organic spinach strawberry salad.
- Most store bought salad dressings contain chemicals and preservatives *The Healthy Edge* suggests to avoid. Making your own salad dressing is a quick and healthy option!

# Balsamic Vinaigrette Salad Dressing

Makes 6 servings
Serving size: 2 Tbsp
Prep time: 5 minutes

## What you'll need:

¼ cup Balsamic vinegar*

½ cup cold pressed extra virgin olive oil

¼ tsp raw agave nectar*

Pinch of sea salt to taste *(optional)*

1. Blend balsamic vinegar, agave, and salt in a blender for 10 seconds.

2. Slowly add olive oil to mixture while blending on low.This helps to emulsify (combine) the mixture.

*Contact manufacturer to ensure product is gluten-free.

### Chef's Serving Suggestions

- This dressing is great on any salad, especially Greek or spinach salads.
- This dressing can also be used on the *Cucumber and Tomato Salad* recipe.

# Sour Cream Substitute

Makes ½ cup
Serving size: 2 Tbsp
Prep time: 3 minutes

## What you'll need:

¼ cup low-fat organic cottage cheese*

¼ cup plain low-fat organic yogurt*

1 tsp organic skim milk

1 Blend all ingredients together until combined well by hand or pulse for a few seconds in a food processor.

*Contact manufacturer to ensure product is gluten-free.*

### Chef's Serving Suggestions

- Add as a topping to your favorite chili.
- Use in wraps and pitas instead of mayonnaise.
- Use when you desire a creamy salad dressing.
- Use in chicken salad instead of mayonnaise.
- Use on anything you would normally use sour cream.

# Tzatziki Sauce

Makes 1¼ cup sauce
Serving Size: 2 Tbsp
Total prep time: 10 minutes

## What you'll need:

2 cups plain low-fat organic yogurt,* divided

2 Tbsp fresh garlic, chopped or pressed

4 tsp fresh lemon juice

½ tsp sea salt

½ English *(seedless)* cucumber, diced and patted dry

1. Blend together 1 cup yogurt and garlic.

2. Transfer to bowl.

3. Whisk in lemon juice, sea salt, and remaining yogurt.

4. Stir in cucumber.

   *Contact manufacturer to ensure product is gluten-free.*

## Chef's Serving Suggestions

- Pat the cucumber dry with a paper towel after dicing. The excess water from the cucumber will make the sauce too thin.
- For a smoother sauce, blend the cucumber in with step 1.
- Serve over roast beef, pork, or lamb.
- Use in pita sandwiches or in wraps.
- Use as a salad dressing or vegetable dip.

# Basil Pesto

Makes 2 cups
Serving size: 2 Tbsp
Prep time: 5 minutes

## What you'll need:

2 cups fresh basil

½ cup fresh grated organic Parmesano Reggiano*

¼ cup raw, unsalted pine nuts*

1 Tbsp fresh garlic, chopped or pressed

¼ tsp sea salt

¾ cup olive oil

**PARMESANO REGGIANO** is true Parmesan cheese. It is high quality and offers a creamy texture to this pesto sauce. You can substitute other less expensive or lower quality Parmesan cheeses, but you may have to use more to achieve a comparable taste. Using Parmesano Reggiano will produce the most flavorful pesto.

**1** Blend together in a food processor or blender until well combined.

*Contact manufacturer to ensure product is gluten-free.*

### Chef's Serving Suggestions

- Use as a pasta sauce for hot or cold pasta sides. Mix 2 Tbsp pesto with ½ cup of 100% whole or sprouted grain pasta. Add some diced tomatoes for a great side dish.
- Use this pesto to make crusted pork loin, *Grilled Mediterranean Flank Steak*, or beef tenderloin.

# Celery Root Puree

Makes 1¼ cups
Serving size: ¼–½ cup
Total prep time: 20 minutes

## What you'll need:

1 tsp onion, minced

2 cups celery root, cubed

½ tsp garlic, minced

⅛ tsp *(or 1 pinch)* sea salt

1 tsp fresh thyme *(1/2 tsp dried)*

Small pinch of ground nutmeg

1⅓ cup low-sodium organic
   chicken stock*

**CELERY ROOT PUREE** pictured with baked salmon

① In a medium sauce pan, combine all ingredients.

② Bring to a boil over medium-high heat. Reduce heat to a very low boil (simmer) for 12 minutes. Stir occasionally.

③ Transfer into a food processor and combine. Serve.

*Contact manufacturer to ensure product is gluten-free.*

### Chef's Serving Suggestions

• Serve under any grilled, baked, broiled, or poached wild caught fish or organic chicken.

• Makes a great side item to any dish.

• Add ½ cup to a small pot of chicken soup to slightly thicken and give extra flavor.

• Try it in your Thanksgiving stuffing too!

# Tomato Caper Sauce

Makes ½ cups
Serving size: 2 Tbsp
Total prep time: 10–12 minutes

 **What you'll need:**

1 tsp olive oil

2 Tbsp onions, minced

1 clove garlic, minced

2 Tbsp capers

1 organic Roma tomato, diced

5 Tbsp low-sodium organic
   chicken or vegetable stock*

¼ tsp sea salt

❶ Heat olive oil in a 6 inch sauté pan on medium-high heat for 1 minute.

❷ Add onions, garlic, and capers. Sauté for 1 minute.

❸ Add tomatoes. Sauté for 1 additional minute.

❹ Add stock. Turn stove burner off.  Stir in salt. Serve.

   *Contact manufacturer to ensure product is gluten-free.*

 **Chef's Serving Suggestions**

- This sauce is great with fish, especially salmon!
- Substitute the capers in this sauce with fresh green peppercorns.  The green peppercorns taste great with meat, but capers are usually preferred if this sauce is served with fish.
- Green peppercorns may be difficult to find, but worth the hunt.  Look for them in specialty shops or larger grocery stores and markets.

# Tomato Mushroom Sauce

Makes 6 servings
Serving size: 2 Tbsp
Prep time: 10 minutes

## What you'll need:

1 cup mushrooms, diced *(about 7 mushroom caps)*

2 organic Roma tomatoes, diced

1 tsp fresh garlic, minced *(1 clove)*

2 tsp olive oil

4 Tbsp low-sodium organic chicken or vegetable stock*

1. Heat olive oil in a 10–12" sauté pan on medium heat for about 1 minute.

2. Add onions and garlic.  Sauté until slightly brown.

3. Add mushrooms and tomatoes.  Cook together for about 30–45 seconds.

4. Add stock and reduce heat to low.  Cover and simmer for about 1 minute.

5. Stir and serve.

   *Contact manufacturer to ensure product is gluten-free.*

### Chef's Serving Suggestions

- Similar to the *Tomato Caper Sauce*, you can add 1½ tsp fresh green peppercorns at step 3.
- This sauce is great served over any broiled fish, especially salmon.
- If you would like this sauce a little thicker, use a bit of organic low-sodium tomato paste.

97

# Marinara Sauce

Makes 5 servings • Serving size: ½ cup
Prep time: 15 minutes
Cook time: 45 minutes to 1 hour

 **What you'll need:**

1 Tbsp olive oil

½ medium onion, chopped or thinly sliced

2 cloves garlic, minced

1 can low-sodium diced organic
tomatoes* *(28 oz.)*

½ cup water

4 sprigs fresh thyme *(1 tsp dried)*

2 sprigs fresh rosemary *(¼ tsp dried)*

3 large basil leaves, whole

¼ tsp sea salt *(as needed)*

1. Heat olive oil on medium to medium-high heat in a medium sized sauce pot.

2. Add onion and sauté 2 minutes.

3. Add garlic and sauté for another 2 minutes.

4. Add tomatoes, water, thyme, rosemary, and basil.

5. Reduce heat to medium–low and simmer 45 minutes to 1 hour, stirring occasionally.

6. Add salt if needed.

7. Remove herb stems and serve.

   *Contact manufacturer to ensure product is gluten-free.*

 **Chef's Serving Suggestions**

- Cool this sauce on the counter for up to 30 minutes, then place in the fridge uncovered until completely cooled. Cover and store.

- This can be stored in the refrigerator up to 5 days or it can be frozen after it is cooled. To thaw, place in refrigerator overnight.

# BBQ Sauce

Makes 3/4 cup
Prep time: 5 minutes

## What you'll need:

½ cup organic ketchup*

¼ cup onions, chopped

2 tsp fresh garlic, chopped or pressed

3 tsp Bragg Liquid Aminos

2 tsp raw agave nectar*

½ tsp Tamari*

½ tsp liquid smoke*

**BRAGG LIQUID AMINOS** is a *Healthy Edge* approved alternative to Worcestershire sauce.

**TAMARI** is a *Healthy Edge* approved alternative to a low-sodium soy sauce.

**①** Blend all ingredients together in food processor.

*Contact manufacturer to ensure product is gluten-free.*

---

 **Chef's Serving Suggestions**

• Add ½ tsp crushed red pepper for some kick.

• Use this sauce to marinate, BBQ, or as a dip.

• Mix with the boiled organic chicken from the *Low-Sodium Chicken Stock* recipe to make BBQ chicken sandwiches or wraps.

# Healthy Holiday Gravy

Makes 5 cups • Serving size: ¼ cup
Prep time: 50 minutes to 1 hour
(largely unattended)

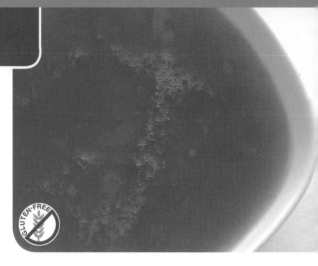

 **What you'll need:**

Turkey gizzards from one organic turkey
*(do not include the liver)*

8 cups low-sodium chicken stock*

2 bay leaves

4 whole mushrooms

2 Tbsp onions, minced

1 clove garlic, minced

1 cup stone ground soy, garbanzo or
100% whole wheat flour *(See Chef's
Suggestions below)*

1¼ cup cold water

 **Chef's Serving Suggestions**

- The stock or gravy base has to boil
  when you add the flour/water mixture.
  The boiling causes the flour starches to
  be released and bind with the mixture
  to make the gravy thicken.

- If using 100% whole wheat flour, reduce
  to ¼ cup and add more as needed.

- To make gluten-free, use stone ground
  soy or garbanzo flour.

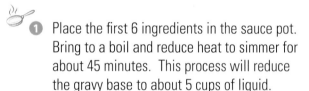

**1** Place the first 6 ingredients in the sauce pot.
Bring to a boil and reduce heat to simmer for
about 45 minutes. This process will reduce
the gravy base to about 5 cups of liquid.

**2** Pour gravy base through a fine strainer or
sieve, and transfer the strained liquid base to
a clean sauce pot. Return to a light boil.

**3** In a separate bowl, mix flour and water
together with a whisk until there are no
clumps.

**4** As gravy base is boiling, whisk in the flour/
water mixture until it forms the gravy
consistency your family desires. (You may
not need to use all of the flour/water mixture
you prepared.)

**5** Remove from heat and serve.

*Contact manufacturer to ensure product is gluten-
free.*

# Black Bean & Garlic Spread

Makes 1 cup
Total time: 5 minutes

## What you'll need:

1 cup pre-cooked or canned low-sodium
  black beans* *(15 oz.)*

½ tsp garlic

1. Drain and rinse black beans if using canned.

2. Combine beans and garlic together in food processor.

   *Contact manufacturer to ensure product is gluten-free.*

### Chef's Serving Suggestions

- This can be used when baking fish like hake, halibut or salmon. Not recommended on tuna steak. Fresh tuna steak has a more delicate taste and this spread would over-power the tuna.

- You can use this spread when baking chicken. After searing, spread on the organic chicken before placing in the oven to bake.

## SHEDDING THE BABY WEIGHT

**MY HEALTHY EDGE JOURNEY STARTED 6 MONTHS AGO. I WAS AT A POINT IN MY LIFE THAT I KNEW I NEEDED TO FOCUS ON MY HEALTH.** At the age of 25 I was

overweight and had borderline high blood pressure. After having my son 3 years ago, I got "stuck in a rut" with my lifestyle. I didn't think I ate that badly but I didn't have the energy or motivation to do anything.

At the beginning of this year I was motivated to lose weight because of a desire to have another child. So with nearly all the baby weight from my first child to lose and a blood pressure problem, I decided to try a well-known weight loss program. I lost 10 pounds, but soon realized that I may lose the weight but my overall health would stay the same because of the types of foods I was still eating.

Going through *The Healthy Edge* was an amazing journey. I loved how *The Healthy Edge* helped my health physically, mentally and emotionally.

**BEFORE**

I began making changes in what I decided to put into my body right away.

It wasn't until about week four that I also made changes in the food that I was buying for my husband and son. I knew they needed to go on this health journey, too. The changes were not an easy thing to do, but I knew the long term benefits and that made it worth the effort.

I also started exercising routinely. I found that I started to really enjoy it and over time I saw my athletic ability improving. I never thought that eight weeks could change my life forever, but it did.

**AFTER**

Now, 6 months later, I have released over 25 pounds. I have officially released all my baby weight. I am wearing clothes out of old boxes that I never thought I would ever get to wear again. I am living *The Healthy Edge* and taking a quality supplement every day. I feel great! My mood has improved and I look as healthy as I feel.

For the first time in my life I feel stress free about my weight and feel a sense of freedom when it comes to eating that I have never felt. I may have done the work to get where I am today but without *The Healthy Edge* I would never have had the energy or the willpower. *The Healthy Edge* provided the tools I needed to take control of my life.

My goals are to continue implementing changes in my life and in those of my family. We are looking forward to getting pregnant and having a pregnancy free from complications. I am also supporting other people to change their lives and their health by sharing with them *The Healthy Edge*. I am now the example they can look up to and follow.

We only get one body and one life and I have chosen to live my life abundantly!

JAN GRIEVES, USA
**RELEASED 25 POUNDS**

# April's Favorite Easy Chicken

Makes two 6–7 oz. chicken breasts
Serving size: 1 chicken breast
Prep time: 5 minutes • Bake time: 30 minutes

 **What you'll need:**

2 organic chicken breasts 6–7 oz. each

½ tsp fresh thyme *(1/4 tsp dried)*

½ tsp fresh rosemary *(1/4 tsp dried)*

¼ tsp sea salt

2 tsp coconut oil

Olive oil or olive oil cooking spray

**APRIL LOVES THIS RECIPE** because it is so easy, quick and tasty! You don't have to sacrifice taste when eating healthy.

❶ Preheat oven to 350° and prepare a broiler pan with olive oil or spray.

❷ Combine together thyme, rosemary, and salt.

❸ Divide spice mixture in half.

❹ Sprinkle each chicken breast with ½ of the spice mixture.

❺ Heat coconut oil in a 12" pan over medium-high heat.

❻ Brown the chicken breasts together in pan for 1 minute on each side. Transfer to broiler pan.

❼ Place in oven for 30 minutes or until the center of the chicken reaches 165°.

# Cabbage Baked Chicken

Makes 2 servings • Serving size: 1 chicken breast
Prep time: 10 minutes or less
Cook time: 30–40 minutes

## What you'll need:

½ tsp fresh thyme *(1/4 dried)*

½ tsp fresh rosemary *(1/4 dried)*

¼ tsp sea salt

½ tsp olive oil

2 organic chicken breasts *(6–7 oz. each)*

2 large green cabbage leaves

8 toothpicks or 2 kabob skewers

1. Preheat oven to 350° and prepare a broiler pan with olive oil or spray.

2. Combine thyme, rosemary, and salt.

3. Divide spice mixture in half.

4. Rub both sides of each chicken breast with ½ of the spice mixture.

5. Place each chicken breast onto 1 cabbage leaf.

6. Wrap cabbage around chicken and hold in place with toothpicks (may take 4 toothpicks for each piece of chicken, or 1 kabob skewer).

7. Place on broiler pan in the oven for 30 minutes or until the center of the chicken reaches 165°.

### Chef's Serving Suggestions

- Double this recipe for larger families!
- Serve with fresh organic tomato slices and drizzle with some aged Balsamic vinegar.
- Try this with the *Asparagus and Tomato Half-Casserole* or the *Mediterranean Zucchini* recipes.

# Chicken Pineapple Fajitas

Makes 8 servings
Serving size: ½ cup each
Prep and cook time: under 20 minutes

 **What you'll need:**

2 tsp coconut oil

2 – 6–8 oz. organic chicken breasts *(cut into small strips or cubes)*

3 cloves fresh garlic, chopped

1 onion, sliced or chopped

1 organic green or red bell pepper, chopped

½ tsp onion powder

½ tsp garlic powder

⅛ tsp paprika

¼ tsp chili powder

¾ tsp ground cumin

⅛ tsp ground red cayenne pepper *(optional, spicy)*

¼ tsp sea salt

1½ cups fresh pineapple chunks

8 Tbsp *(3/4 cup)* organic low-fat plain yogurt* *(optional)*

¾ cup fresh organic tomatoes, diced

Fresh cilantro to garnish *(optional)*

❶ Heat coconut oil in a 12" sauté pan on medium-high.

❷ As the oil just begins to ripple add chicken and sauté for 1 minute.

❸ Add garlic, onions, peppers, spices, and sauté for 3 minutes.

❹ Stir in pineapple, reduce heat to a simmer, cover, and let stand for 2 minutes or until chicken is fully cooked. It may take longer if chicken was cut large.

*Contact manufacturer to ensure product is gluten-free.*

---

### Chef's Serving Suggestions

- Serve ½ cup on a 100% whole grain or sprouted grain tortilla and top with 1 Tbsp low-fat plain or Greek style organic yogurt and fresh diced organic tomatoes.

- Serve over a bed of organic greens for a tasty salad. This makes this recipe gluten and dairy free!

# Chicken Portobello

Makes 4 servings • Serving size: ½ Portobello mushroom & ½ chicken breast
Prep time: 15 minutes • Cook time: 1 hour

## What you'll need:

2 large Portobello mushrooms, stems removed

2 cups organic baby spinach, chopped

2 organic chicken breasts, 6 oz. each

2 tsp fresh rosemary, chopped *(1 tsp dried)*

½ tsp sea salt, divided

2 cups marinara sauce *(see Marinara Sauce recipe)*

2 Tbsp fresh grated organic Parmesan cheese\* *(optional)*

1. Pre-heat oven to 350°.

2. Line a deep casserole dish with parchment paper.

3. Place mushrooms upside down in bottom of dish.

4. Fill each mushroom with 1 cup spinach.

5. Top each mushroom with 1 chicken breast on top of the spinach.

6. Sprinkle each chicken breast with 1 tsp rosemary and ¼ tsp salt.

7. Pour marinara sauce over chicken.

8. Bake 1 hour.

9. Pull out 5–7 minutes before end time, sprinkle with Parmesan cheese and continue to bake for remaining 5–7 minutes.

10. Remove from oven and cool 5 minutes. Cut each in half and serve.

   *\*Contact manufacturer to ensure product is gluten-free.*

 **Chef's Serving Suggestions**

- If you don't have marinara sauce on hand, mix 1 can low-sodium diced organic tomatoes,\* 1 clove garlic minced, ½ tsp sea salt, and ½ tsp oregano. Divide mixture over the two chicken Portobellos and continue to step 8.

# Chicken & Asparagus with Noodles

Makes 2 servings • Serving size: ½ chicken
breast and 1¼ cup veggies
Total prep time: under 30 minutes

## What you'll need:

1 tsp coconut oil

1 organic chicken breast, cubed or sliced

3 Tbsp onions, chopped

2 cloves garlic, minced

2 cups asparagus, coarsely chopped

¼ tsp sea salt

1 can low-sodium diced organic tomatoes
   *(or 2 diced organic Roma tomatoes)*

1½ cup pre-cooked sprouted whole
   grain or 100% whole wheat noodles

½ cup black olives, pitted *(optional)*

1. In a 12" pan, heat oil over medium-high heat. Add chicken breast and sauté for about 3 minutes.

2. Add onions and garlic. Sauté for another 2 minutes.

3. Add asparagus, salt, tomatoes and sauté together for 3 minutes.

4. Remove from heat and stir in noodles and black olives (if using), then serve.

### Chef's Serving Suggestions

- This can be a 20 minute meal. Start cooking the noodles when you begin prepping all the other ingredients. For quick prep, keep diced onions and garlic on hand and have the veggies in your fridge washed and ready to be used.

- Double this recipe and cook in a wok for the whole family.

- An alternative to noodles is quinoa, barley or sweet brown rice. Using quinoa or sweet brown rice would make this recipe gluten-free.

# Sunday Baked Chicken

**Makes 1 chicken
Serving size: 4–6 oz.
Total prep time: 3 hours 15 minutes**

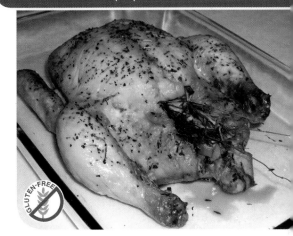

## What you'll need:

1 whole organic chicken

4 sprigs fresh thyme

4 sprigs fresh rosemary

1 organic apple, quartered *(optional)*

½ onion, quartered *(optional)*

2 stalks organic celery, cut into thirds *(optional)*

1 tsp olive oil

½ tsp sea salt

Olive oil or olive oil cooking spray

❶ Preheat oven to 300° and lightly coat broiler pan with olive oil or cooking spray.

❷ Stuff chicken with the apple, onion, celery (if using), and two whole sprigs each of the rosemary and thyme.

❸ Remove thyme and rosemary from remaining sprigs. Chop rosemary and mix with thyme and salt.

❹ Rub olive oil onto chicken skin. Rub the salt and remaining rosemary and thyme onto chicken skin.

❺ Bake for 3 hours. Internal temperature should reach 165–175°.

## Chef's Serving Suggestions

- Prepare this a day in advance and refrigerate until you are ready to bake it. Toss it in after breakfast on Sunday and have a fresh baked chicken for lunch.

- It is healthiest to avoid eating the chicken skin, but baking with it on helps the bird maintain the moisture needed for a tender and delicious serving.

- In the above picture, the rosemary and thyme shown on the outside of the chicken were first chopped and then rubbed on prior to baking. You can chop the herbs or leave them whole.

- For a really quick fix, skip the stuffing ingredients and just rub the chicken with olive oil, sea salt, and 2 sprigs each of the herbs and bake according to the directions.

# Oat Crusted Chicken breast

Makes two 6–7 oz. chicken breasts
Serving size: 1 chicken breast
Prep time: 10 minutes • Bake time: 30 minutes

## What you'll need:

½ cup whole oats*

1 Tbsp fresh thyme *(1/2 Tbsp dried)*

½ tsp sea salt

2 organic chicken breasts, 6–7 oz. each

2 tsp coconut oil

Olive oil or olive oil cooking spray

1. Combine together oats, thyme, and salt in a shallow dish.

2. Preheat oven to 350° and prepare a broiler pan with olive oil or spray or parchment paper.

3. Roll each chicken breast in mixture until well covered.

4. Heat coconut oil in a 12" pan on medium-high heat.

5. Put both chicken breasts in pan and brown for 1 minute on each side.

6. Transfer chicken to broiler pan, then place in oven for 30 minutes or until the center of the chicken reaches 165°.

*Contact manufacture to ensure product is gluten-free.*

 **Chef's Serving Suggestions**

• Double or triple this recipe for a larger family.

# Indian Curry Chicken (or Pork)

Makes 6 Servings • Serving size: 1½ cups
Prep time: 10 minutes • Cook time: 20 minutes

## What you'll need:

3 Tbsp olive oil

1 cup organic chicken breast or pork loin, cut into 1 inch cubes

4 cloves fresh garlic, chopped or pressed

¾ cup onion, chopped

11 whole dried cloves

1 cinnamon stick

4 cups low-sodium chicken stock

¾ tsp curry powder

2 cups 100% whole grain orzo pasta or pearl barley *(see Chef's Suggestions)*

❶ Heat olive oil in a 12" sauté pan over medium-high heat and add meat, garlic, and onion.

❷ Sauté for 4 minutes, then add cloves, cinnamon, stock, curry, and orzo pasta.

❸ Stir together. Bring to a boil. Reduce to medium heat, cover and cook for 10 minutes, stirring occasionally.

❹ Turn off heat and remove lid. Allow to sit, uncovered for 5 minutes. Remove cloves and cinnamon stick before serving.

### Chef's Serving Suggestions

- 100% whole grain orzo pasta can sometimes be a challenge to find. Substitute 2 cups rinsed pearl barley for the orzo. Increase cook time from 10 to 15 minutes.

- Make gluten-free: substitute 5 cups pre-cooked brown basmati rice for the orzo. To make this substitution, reduce stock to 1 cup, reduce cook time to 6-8 minutes, and follow all other directions as stated.

# Mango Chicken & Beans

Makes 5½ cups • Serving size: 2 cups
Prep time: 10 minutes • Cook: 10 minutes

 **What you'll need:**

1½ tsp coconut oil

1 mango, peeled and cubed

1 clove garlic, minced

½ medium onion, sliced

¾ cup black beans*

¾ cup black-eyed peas

1 cup organic chicken, pre-cooked

1 cup bean sprouts

3 cups organic baby Romaine or spring mix greens

1. In a large skillet, heat oil over medium-high heat.

2. Add onions and garlic. Sauté for 1–2 minutes.

3. Add mango and sauté until slightly browned, about 2–3 minutes.

4. Add beans, chicken, bean sprouts, and baby Romaine lettuce. Stir until Romaine is wilted and the chicken is heated throughout, about 3–5 minutes. Serve.

*Contact manufacture to ensure product is gluten-free.*

 **Chef's Serving Suggestions**

• This can be a complete meal or you can use it to stuff a sprouted or 100% whole grain wrap or pita.

• Add a dollop of low-fat plain organic yogurt for added flavor.

# Squash & Chicken with Pasta

Makes 2 cups • Serving size: 1 cup
Prep time: 5 minutes
Cook time: under 10 minutes

## What you'll need:

1 tsp olive oil

¾ cup small cubed kabocha or buttercup squash

2 Tbsp red onions, minced

½ cup low-sodium chicken stock*

1 organic Roma tomato, diced

¼ cup cubed, pre-cooked organic chicken or turkey

¾ cup pre-cooked 100% whole grain or sprouted grain pasta *(To make dish gluten-free, see Chef's Suggestions.)*

¼ tsp sea salt

1 Heat olive oil in a large skillet on medium-high heat.

2 Add squash and brown for 2–3 minutes.

3 Add onions and continue to sauté for 1 more minute.

4 Add stock, tomato, chicken, salt, and pasta.

5 Stir together for 3–5 minutes until chicken is heated throughout.

### Chef's Serving Suggestions

• Serve topped with chopped raw, unsalted pine nuts and fresh chives instead of cheese!

• Serve this dish with pre-cooked brown basmati rice or quinoa for a tasty gluten-free dish!

# Spaghetti Squash & Chicken Casserole

Makes 6 servings
Prep time: 15 minutes
Cook time: 1 hour unattended

 **What you'll need:**

5 cups cooked spaghetti squash *(see recipe for Spaghetti Squash)*

2 pounds green asparagus, washed and ends cut off

1½ Tbsp olive oil

4–6 oz. organic chicken breasts, 6 oz., cut in half

2 tsp sea salt

2 *(28 oz)* cans of low-sodium diced organic tomatoes*

2 Tbsp fresh thyme, chopped *(1 Tbsp dried)*

2 Tbsp fresh rosemary, chopped *(1 Tbsp dried)*

4 cloves garlic, chopped

Olive oil or olive oil cooking spray

 **Chef's Serving Suggestions**

- Use 4 cups organic baby spinach in place of asparagus. Prepare dish as directed above.
- Garnish with 2 tsp freshly grated organic Parmesan cheese* per serving.

❶ Preheat oven to 350°. Lightly brush or spray a 9"x13" glass casserole dish with olive oil.

❷ Spread squash into bottom of casserole dish.

❸ Place asparagus side by side across squash.

❹ Drizzle 1 Tbsp olive oil over asparagus.

❺ Rub or sprinkle ¼ tsp salt onto each chicken breast half. Place chicken over asparagus.

❻ Pour diced tomatoes over chicken.

❼ Combine thyme, rosemary, and garlic and evenly sprinkle mixture over top.

❽ Bake approximately 1 hour or until chicken center reaches 165°.

*Contact manufacture to ensure product is gluten-free.*

# Quick Chicken Pasta

Makes 2 servings
Serving size: 2 cups
Prep time: 10 minutes

## What you'll need:

2 tsp olive oil

2 Tbsp onions, diced or minced

1 cup cooked organic chicken *(or organic turkey)*

2 organic Roma tomatoes, diced

1 cup pre-cooked 100% whole grain or sprouted noodles *(penne)*

½ tsp sea salt

½ cup organic baby spinach *(or organic baby arugula)*, chopped

2 Tbsp raw, unsalted pine nuts or sliced raw, unsalted almonds

1 Heat olive oil in pan on medium high heat for 1 minute. Add onions and sauté for 20 seconds.

2 Add turkey and tomatoes and sauté for 1 minute.

3 Add noodles and salt and sauté for 1 minute.

4 Remove from heat and stir in spinach and nuts. Serve right away.

### Chef's Serving Suggestions

- You can top with 1 Tbsp fresh grated organic Parmesan* or crumbled organic feta cheese.*

- This is a great quick lunch or dinner.

- Make this dish gluten-free by using pre-cooked quinoa, sweet brown rice or other gluten-free grains.

# Not Just for Thanksgiving Turkey

Makes 12 servings • Serving size: 6–8 oz.
Prep time: 10 minutes • Cook time: about 3 hours

 **What you'll need:**

1 organic turkey *(12–14 lbs)*

10 sprigs fresh thyme

10 sprigs fresh rosemary

½ tsp sea salt

¼ tsp fresh thyme, chopped *(1/8 dried)*

¼ tsp fresh rosemary, chopped *(1/8 dried)*

Olive oil or olive oil cooking spray

❶ Preheat oven to 300° and prepare turkey roasting pan and rack with a light coating of olive oil or olive oil cooking spray. (Line the pan with parchment paper for easier clean up).

❷ Unpack the turkey over the sink to catch any unexpected drippings.

❸ Remove gizzards (do not discard; you can use these for gravy).

❹ Rinse turkey off and pat dry with paper towels.

❺ Place the turkey on the rack in the turkey roasting pan, breast up.

❻ Stuff turkey with thyme and rosemary sprigs.

❼ Rub skin with olive oil.

❽ Sprinkle salt and chopped herbs evenly over turkey.

❾ Bake uncovered for 4 hours 15 minutes, or until timer pops up. Do not baste!

❿ Remove from oven and allow turkey to rest 20–30 minutes before carving, so the meat is more tender and juicy. Internal temperature should reach 165–175°.

 **Chef's Serving Suggestions**

- Plan on one pound of turkey per person for holiday dinners.

- Bake a turkey once a month to have plenty of lean meat to store in the freezer for quick meals. Buying a whole turkey is much more economical than buying turkey cutlets.

- Leftovers make great soups, chili, salads, wraps, and can be used in any of *The Healthy Edge* recipes that call for pre-cooked organic chicken or turkey.

- Same rules apply when shopping for turkey as if you were shopping for chicken. Buy organic!

# Mango-Squash with Turkey Breast

Makes 2 servings • Serving size: 1½ cups
Prep time: 10 minutes • Cook time: 10 minutes

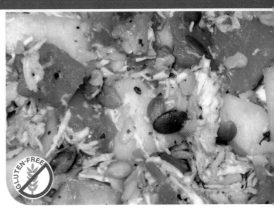

## What you'll need:

1 cup buttercup or kabocha squash, peeled, seeds removed, and cubed

1 tsp coconut oil

2 Tbsp red onions, minced

¾ cup low-sodium chicken or vegetable stock*

1 cup pre-cooked brown rice

1 tsp fresh marjoram *(1/2 tsp dried)*

2 Tbsp raw, unsalted pumpkin seeds

1 mango, cubed in large chunks

½ cup pre-cooked organic turkey or chicken, diced

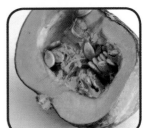

**KABOCHA SQUASH**

❶ In a large skillet, heat coconut oil over medium-high heat.

❷ Add squash and sauté 2 minutes.

❸ Add onions and sauté for about another minute.

❹ Stir in stock, brown rice, marjoram, pumpkin seeds. Cook for 5–6 minutes stirring occasionally. As mixture boils, reduce heat to medium.

❺ Stir in mango and turkey. Heat for 2–5 minutes and serve.

*Contact manufacture to ensure product is gluten-free.*

## 🍳 Chef's Serving Suggestions

- This dish is great with ½ tsp Curry powder mixed in at step 4.
- Use some crushed red or cayenne pepper for added spice.
- Great for a quick lunch or dinner.
- Add ½ cup pre-cooked black beans at step 5, for added protein and fiber.
- If you are using good chicken or vegetable stock, you may not need to add any salt to this recipe.

# Turkey Burgers

Makes 10 servings • Serving size: 5 oz. burgers
Prep time: 10 minutes
Cook time: varies (approx 10 minutes on hot grill)

## What you'll need:

1 onion

3 cloves fresh garlic, minced

1 tsp fresh marjoram or oregano, chopped
  *(1/2 tsp dried)*

1 tsp fresh thyme, chopped *(1/2 tsp dried)*

½ tsp Tamari sauce*

½ tsp Bragg Liquid Aminos

3 lbs lean organic ground turkey

1 Combine all ingredients except turkey in a food processor.

2 Add pureed mixture to meat. Use clean bare hands to mix well.

3 Portion into 5 oz. balls and form patties.

4 Cook turkey burgers on the grill.

5 Remember that turkey, unlike beef, must be FULLY cooked before serving (165° in center).

*Contact manufacture to ensure product is gluten-free.*

 **Chef's Serving Suggestions**

- Burgers can be wrapped and refrigerated for up to 24 hours or frozen up to 1 month. This storage time is taking into consideration that you are using fresh ground turkey.

- Pre-frozen ground turkey should be used within 24 hours of thawing.

- These are good enough to eat by themselves or on 100% whole grain or sprouted bread! Check out the sauces and dips for some great toppings!

# Turkey Chili

Makes 6 servings • Serving size: 1½ cups
Prep Time: 10 minutes
Crock pot cook time: 4–7 hours

## What you'll need:

2 lbs lean ground organic turkey

1 onion, chopped

1 can low-sodium diced organic tomatoes* *(28 oz.)*

5 cups low-sodium chicken or vegetable stock*

½ tsp dried oregano

3 Tbsp chili powder

1 tsp ground cumin

2 cloves fresh garlic, chopped

3 whole bay leaves

2 tsp sea salt

¾ cup dried small red beans *(pre-soaked overnight)*

¾ cup dried red kidney beans *(pre-soaked overnight)*

¾ cup dried Roman beans *(pre-soaked overnight)*

¼ tsp crushed red pepper (optional)

① Brown turkey and onions in a 12" skillet.

② Transfer turkey and onions to crock pot and add remaining ingredients.

③ Cook in crock pot on high setting for 4 hours or low setting for 6–7 hours.

*Contact manufacture to ensure product is gluten-free.*

---

 **Chef's Serving Suggestions**

- If you choose to use drained and rinsed canned low-sodium beans* instead of dried beans, reduce the salt to 1 tsp, reduce the chicken stock to 2 cups, and reduce to 2 hours on high or 4½–5½ hours on low.

- You can also prepare this on the stove in a large pot in about 45 minutes using canned low-sodium beans or just under 2 hours with pre-soaked dried beans.

# Quick Turkey Chili

Makes 4 servings
Serving size: 2 cups each
Prep and cook time: 30 minutes

## What you'll need:

1 lb organic lean ground turkey

1 onion, chopped

2 cloves fresh garlic, chopped

1 can low-sodium diced organic tomatoes* *(28 oz.)*

2 cans low-sodium red kidney beans* *(drained and rinsed)*

1 cup water

2 whole bay leaves

2 tsp ground cumin

1 Tbsp chili powder

1 tsp sea salt

1 organic green bell pepper, chopped

❶ Brown ground turkey, onions, and garlic in medium or large stock pot on medium-high heat.

❷ Add remaining ingredients except for chopped bell peppers.

❸ Turn heat up and bring mixture almost to boiling point. Cover and reduce heat to medium-low for 10 minutes. Stir occasionally.

❹ Stir in chopped bell peppers and cook for an additional 10 minutes.

*Contact manufacture to ensure product is gluten-free.*

## Chef's Serving Suggestions

- For larger families, increase serving size by adding another 28 oz. can of low-sodium diced organic tomatoes,* 2 cans of low-sodium beans* (drained and rinsed), 1 cup water, and up to 1 cup frozen green beans. Increase cook time 5–10 minutes.

- Substitute lean ground organic turkey with ground organic chicken breast.

- Serve this chili topped with ½ diced fresh cayenne pepper (with seeds) for a HOT and delicious meal!

- Add 1 Tbsp organic low-fat plain or Greek style yogurt* to each serving to add creamy smoothness.

# Quick Southwestern Chili

Makes 8 servings • Serving size: 1½ cups
Prep and cook time: approximately 30 minutes

## What you'll need:

1 lb organic, grass fed beef combined with 1 lb organic ground turkey

1 onion, chopped

2 cloves fresh garlic, chopped

3 cans low-sodium diced organic tomatoes* (14 oz. each)

1 can mild green chilies* (4–5 oz.)

1 organic green bell pepper, chopped

1 organic red bell pepper, chopped

2 cans low-sodium black beans* (drained and rinsed)

1 cup frozen whole-kernel corn

1 cup water

1 Tbsp ground cumin

1 Tbsp chili powder

1 tsp dried oregano

1 tsp sea salt

 **Chef's Serving Suggestions**

- You can use 1 lb ground beef combined with 1 lb ground turkey.
- Serve this chili topped with:
  Low or non-fat organic shredded cheddar cheese.*
  A dollop of low-fat plain or Greek style organic yogurt*
  Fresh cilantro, chopped
  Fresh chives, chopped

**1** In a medium or large stock pot, brown the ground turkey or ground beef with onions and garlic over medium-high heat.

**2** Add remaining ingredients and stir.

**3** Bring mixture to just before boiling, cover and reduce heat to medium-low for 20 minutes.

*Contact manufacture to ensure product is gluten-free.

# One Pot Pork Dinner

Makes 6 servings • Serving size: 2½ cups
Total prep time: 1 hour 15 minutes
(largely unattended)

## What you'll need:

1 tsp olive oil

1 organic pork tenderloin, 12–16 oz.

8 cups low-sodium chicken stock*

1 cup uncooked brown rice, rinsed

2 cups frozen edamame

1 cup carrots, coarsely chopped

2 cups organic spinach or arugula
leaves, chopped

3 organic Roma tomatoes, diced

1. In a large stock pot, heat olive oil on medium-high heat.

2. Brown the pork tenderloin on all sides.

3. Add chicken stock, brown rice, edamame, and carrots. Bring to a boil, reduce heat to medium-low and cover. Cook for 1 hour stirring occasionally (2–3 times).

4. Pull out the pork with tongs and place on a cutting board. Cut into smaller chunks and put back into pot.

5. Place 1/2 cup chopped spinach in the bottom of each serving dish. Ladle out each portion on top of the fresh spinach. Top with fresh organic tomatoes.

   *Contact manufacture to ensure product is gluten-free.*

### Chef's Serving Suggestions

- You will not need to add any additional seasoning or salt to this dish if you use a good chicken stock.

- Add some hot curry sauce for added kick.

- Freeze in airtight containers for up to a month.

- Add another 2 cups of veggies and 1 more cup of chicken stock to increase the serving size to 8.

- You can also prepare in a crock pot. Cook on low for about 6 hours.

# Pork Tenderloin with Apples

Makes 4 servings • Serving size: 4–6 oz. pork and ¾ cup sauce • Prep time: 20–30 minutes
Marinate time: 2+ hours • Cook time: under 30 min.

## What you'll need:

1 organic pork tenderloin *(1 to 1½ lbs and excess fat removed)*, cut into 4 oz. pieces

1½ cups natural, unsweetened apple juice *(divided)*

1 tsp coconut oil

1 cup raw, unsalted walnut halves or pieces

2 organic Gala apples, cut into cubes or sliced

¼ tsp sea salt

**1** Marinate pork tenderloin pieces in 1 cup apple juice for at least 2 hours. Keep refrigerated.

**2** Pre-heat oven to 350°.

**3** Heat coconut oil in large sauté pan on medium-high heat.

**4** Sear pork pieces on all sides. (Use caution! The natural sugars from the apple juice may burn quickly.)

### Chef's Serving Suggestions

• This may sound a little complicated, but it really is easy. Give it a shot and you will be happy you did. Especially you meat lovers!

• This is a great dish to serve when introducing family and friends to low-glycemic cooking. Show them healthy food can and does taste amazing!

• Serve this with steamed broccoli, carrots, and brown rice!

**5** Transfer seared pork pieces to broiler pan and place in oven for 15–20 minutes. Pork is fully cooked when internal temperature is 160–170°.

**6** Utilizing the same pan the pork was seared in (do not wash or rinse between uses), add apples and sear on medium-high heat for 2 minutes. You can add another ½ tsp coconut or olive oil if necessary.

**7** Add walnuts and sauté in pan for additional 1–2 minutes.

**8** Add remaining apple juice and turn off heat. Allow pan to sit on stove until pork is cooked. Serve the apple and walnut sauce over the pork tenderloin.

# Napa Pork Casserole

Makes 4 serving • Serving size: 1¾ cups
Prep time: 10 minutes • Cook time: 1 hour

## What you'll need:

½ head Napa cabbage, sliced into 1 inch thick slices

2 cups whole mushrooms

⅔ cup fresh or frozen green peas

10 slices organic pork tenderloin, 1 oz. each

2 cups organic baby arugula or spinach leaves

3 cups marinara sauce* *(see recipe for Marinara Sauce)*

6 oz. fresh organic mozzarella,* diced or shredded low-fat organic mozzarella*

**PREP BEFORE ADDING
MARINARA SAUCE AND CHEESE**

① Preheat oven to 350°.

② Slice cabbage and layer in bottom of casserole dish.

③ Layer the mushrooms, peas, pork, and arugula or spinach leaves.

④ Cover with marinara sauce and sprinkle mozzarella cheese on top.

⑤ Bake uncovered for 1 hour.

*Contact manufacture to ensure product is gluten-free.*

 **Chef's Serving Suggestions**

- There will be about a cup of extra liquid in the pan after cooking. This is normal liquid release from the marinara and cabbage.

- If you don't have *The Healthy Edge Marinara Sauce* on hand, you can substitute with this quick mixture: 2 cans low-sodium diced organic tomatoes,* 2 tsp fresh thyme (or 1 tsp dried), 2 tsp fresh rosemary (or 1 tsp dried), and 3 cloves fresh minced garlic.

# Stuffed Pork Loin

Makes 5 servings • Serving size: 6 oz.
Prep time: 10–15 minutes
Cook time: 45 minutes to 1 hour

## What you'll need:

2 pounds organic pork loin, trimmed *(excess fat removed)*

1 tsp fresh rosemary, chopped *(1/2 tsp dried)*

2 Tbsp whole oats

2 Tbsp dried cranberries *(watch ingredients)*

2 tsp olive oil

2 Tbsp Ezekiel bread crumbs *(100% whole or sprouted grain bread)*

¼ tsp sea salt

2 tsp coconut oil

Olive oil or olive oil cooking spray

❶ Pre-heat oven to 350°.

❷ Lightly coat broiler pan with olive oil or spray or line with parchment paper.

❸ Cut pork loin lengthwise to open up the middle (as if you were slicing bread for a sub sandwich). Avoid cutting all the way through, you will be stuffing and folding the meat.

❹ Mix together rosemary, oats, cranberries, olive oil, and bread crumbs.

❺ Stuff pork with mixture and close the pork over stuffing.

❻ Heat coconut oil in a 12" sauté pan on medium-high heat.

❼ Sprinkle outside of pork with salt and rub in.

❽ Quick sear the pork for about 1 minute on each side, then transfer to the broiler pan and bake in oven for 45–50 minutes. Internal temperature should be 160–170°.

❾ Remove and cool for 2–3 minutes before cutting.

### Chef's Serving Suggestions

- To make the bread crumbs, toast 1 slice Ezekiel bread, then cool. Place in blender or food processor for 10–20 seconds. (One slice makes about 2 Tbsp bread crumbs.)

- Serve with veggies for a complete meal.

# Stuffed Red Peppers

Makes 4 servings • Serving Size: ½ stuffed pepper
with ¾ cup noodles • Prep time: 15 minutes
Cook time: 50 minutes

 **What you'll need:**

3 cups cooked 100% whole or sprouted
   grain pasta

1½ tsp olive oil

2 organic red bell peppers *(can also use
   yellow or orange)*

1 cup snow peas

8 oz. organic, grass fed beef tenderloin,
   cut into 4 segments

2½ cups marinara sauce *(see recipe for
   Marinara Sauce)*

1 oz. fresh organic mozzarella cheese,
   cut into 4 thin slices

1. Pre-heat oven to 350°.

2. Toss cooked pasta with olive oil and place
   in bottom of 9 inch square baking dish or
   oblong shaped casserole dish.

3. Cut peppers in half, remove seeds and
   place on top of the bed of noodles.

4. Place ¼ cup snow peas inside each pepper.

5. Top the snow peas with one piece of beef
   per pepper.

6. Cover everything with marinara sauce.

7. Top each pepper with a slice of mozzarella
   cheese.

8. Bake uncovered for 50 minutes.

 **Chef's Serving Suggestions**

- If you don't have *The Healthy Edge*
  Marinara Sauce on hand, use this
  mixture as a substitute: Mix together
  1 can diced organic tomatoes, 1 tsp
  fresh thyme (1/2 tsp dried), 1 tsp fresh
  rosemary (1/2 tsp  dried), and 2 fresh
  minced garlic cloves.

- This dish can be prepared up to a day
  ahead of time.  Remove from the fridge
  and let it sit out for 5–8 minutes while
  pre-heating the oven.  Bake as directed.

- To make this dish gluten-free, use a
  gluten-free pasta such as quinoa or
  brown rice pasta.

# Not Your Mom's Meatloaf

Makes 2 meatloaves • 1 loaf makes 4 servings
Serving size: 2 slices (about 6 oz.)
Prep time: 30 minutes • Cook time: 1 hour

## What you'll need:

3 carrots, diced or shredded

1 lb grass fed, organic lean ground beef

1 lb organic lean ground turkey

1 can low-sodium diced or crushed organic tomatoes*

1 onion, diced

1 organic bell pepper *(green, red, or yellow)*, diced

1½ cups whole oats*

2 organic eggs

1 tsp sea salt

2 cups cooked lentils

1. Place diced carrots in a pot of boiling water for 3–5 minutes to soften them while you are mixing other ingredients.

2. Preheat oven to 350° and line a 13"x 9" glass or stoneware baking dish with parchment paper. Place another piece of parchment paper on the counter top.

3. Mix all other ingredients together in a large bowl. It is best to do this with clean bare hands to be sure it is mixed well.

4. When carrots are lightly steamed, drain and add to mixture.

5. Remove mixture from bowl and place onto the extra piece of parchment. Divide mixture in half. Form 2 loaves.

6. Place one loaf in baking dish and place in the oven. Bake 1 hour.

7. Wrap the other meatloaf with the parchment paper, then wrap with plastic wrap or foil and freeze for another day.

*Contact manufacturer to ensure product is gluten-free.*

### Chef's Serving Suggestions

- Serve this meatloaf recipe with steamed broccoli or asparagus and one of *The Healthy Edge* salads for a complete meal.

- The frozen meatloaf will be good for a couple of months. Thaw for at least 24 hours in the fridge before baking.

- This meatloaf is so good you won't need to drown it in ketchup.

- Pack leftovers in an insulated thermos bowl for lunch the next day with some veggies. The kids will love it!

# Crock Pot Beef with Black-Eyed Peas

Makes 4 servings • Serving size: 2–3 oz. of beef with ¾ cup bean & barley mixture • Prep time: 15 minutes • Cook time: 1+ hours (largely unattended)

 ## What you'll need:

1 Tbsp coconut oil

4 pieces grass fed, organic beef tenderloin, approx 2–3 ounces each

½ medium onion, chopped

½ cup pearl barley *(use brown rice to make gluten-free)*

1 cup dried black-eyed peas *(pre-soaked for 8–24 hours, then drained)*

5 cups low-sodium stock* *(beef, chicken, or vegetable)*

1 tsp fresh rosemary, chopped *(1/2 tsp dried)*

1 whole bay leaf

3 cups organic baby spinach, coarsely chopped

 ### Chef's Serving Suggestions

- Although the recipe name is *"Crock Pot" Beef with Black-Eyed Peas,* this is a quick stove top version.

- To prepare in a crock pot, add all ingredients except for spinach. Do not need to use coconut oil for this version. Cook on high heat for 2 hours and 30 minutes, or on low setting for 5–6 hours. Add the spinach just before serving to retain maximum taste and nutrients.

- All crock pots cook at different temperatures, so you may need to adjust the cook time slightly.

- Serve with a big green organic salad or some steamed organic veggies to make a complete meal.

- There should be no need for additional salt if you used a quality stock.

1. Heat coconut oil on medium high heat in a sauté pan or large skillet.

2. Sear the beef on high, 10–15 seconds on each side.

3. Add onions. Reduce to medium heat and sauté for 1 minute.

4. Add barley, black eyed peas, and stock. Bring to a boil and then reduce heat to simmer.

5. Add rosemary and bay leaf. Allow to simmer for 45 minutes, gently stirring occasionally.

6. Turn off heat, stir in chopped spinach and allow to stand for 30 seconds before serving. This will allow the spinach to warm and soften.

# Beef Roast

Makes 8 servings • Serving size: 1½ cups
Prep time: 30 minutes
Cook time: 7–8 hours in a crock pot

## What you'll need:

8 cups water or low-sodium stock *(beef or vegetable)*\*

2 whole bay leaves

2½ lbs bottom round grass fed, organic beef roast *(with fat trimmed off)*

1 tsp sea salt

1 tsp fresh cracked black pepper

1 Tbsp coconut oil

1½ cups carrots, chopped into 1 inch segments

1½ cups organic celery, chopped

3 sprigs fresh thyme

3 cloves fresh garlic, chopped

1 onion, coarsely chopped

2½ Tbsp organic tomato paste\*

2 additional cups chopped carrots

2 cups green beans

### Chef's Serving Suggestions

- Adding the additional carrots and beans in the beginning will result in mushy veggies. Add them no more than 2 hours before serving.

- The carrots and green beans will be so good you won't even miss potatoes. You can add a few new potatoes with the carrots and beans if desired.

- *The Healthy Edge* suggests limiting red meat to one time or less per week. This is a great recipe for your "meat" day!

1. Turn crock pot on high and fill with water or stock. Add bay leaves. Cover and allow it to get hot while preparing the meat and veggies.

2. Sprinkle salt and pepper on all sides of roast and rub it in.

3. Add coconut oil to a large hot skillet on medium heat and brown meat for 10 minutes, turning to sear all sides.

4. Remove beef from pan and set aside. Add carrots, thyme, celery, garlic, and onion to pan and sauté for additional 5 minutes.

5. Place beef back into pan and add tomato paste. Sauté for 5 minutes.

6. Transfer everything to the crock pot, cover with lid, and reduce heat to low. Cook for 7 hours on low.

7. Add the additional carrots and green beans 1½ hours before dinner is to be served.

*\*Contact manufacturer to ensure product is gluten-free.*

# Beef & Barley with Edamame

Makes 4 servings • Serving size: ¾ cup
Prep time: under 10 minutes
Cook time: 2 hours 45 minutes

## What you'll need:

½ cup onions, chopped

8 oz. organic, grass–fed beef tenderloin

1 cup edamame

4 cups low-sodium stock *(beef, chicken, or vegetable)*

2 tsp fresh thyme

1 medium organic tomato, diced

½ cup wild rice *(uncooked)*

2 tsp sea salt

1 cup hulled or pearl barley *(uncooked)*

**PEARL BARLEY** is the most common type of barley found in supermarkets. Compared to hulled barley, pearl barley is less nutritious due to the fact some of the germ and outer bran has been ground away. Although it does cook faster, *The Healthy Edge* recommends using hulled or pot barley when possible to take advantage of all the terrific nutrition available in this grain. Barley is a good source of both soluble and insoluble fiber.

❶ Combine all ingredients except edamame in a crock pot on high for 2½ hours.

❷ Stir in edamame.

❸ Turn off and allow dish to simmer for an additional 10 minutes.  Keep dish covered.

 **Chef's Serving Suggestions**

• Serve over a bed of organic spinach or with some freshly diced organic tomatoes.

# Grilled Flank Steak

Makes 4 servings • Serving size: 6 oz. steak
Prep time: 5–10 min. • Marinating time: 4–8 hours
Cook time: 10–20 minutes

## What you'll need:

1.5 pound organic, grass fed flank steak with fat trimmed off

2 sprigs fresh rosemary

2 cloves garlic, chopped

¼ tsp fresh cracked black pepper

4 Tbsp olive oil

**FLANK STEAK** pictured is marinating.

*The Healthy Edge* suggests purchasing grass fed and organic beef. This ensures the animals have not been treated or fed antibiotics, growth hormones or animal byproducts. Grass fed beef has been shown to have less saturated fat and more Omega-3 (healthy) fat than grain fed beef. You can purchase beef from local farmers directly and store bulk amounts in your freezer. This is economical and healthy!

❶ Mix all ingredients together and marinate 4–8 hours before grilling.

❷ Grill 5–10 minutes each side. Cooking 5 minutes on each side will result in rare to medium rare temperature. Increase cook time to your desired temperature.

 **Chef's Serving Suggestions**

• Serve over a bed of organic spinach or with some freshly diced organic tomatoes.

• To serve, cut against the grain for tender portion. Cutting with the grain will result in chewy meat.

# Grilled Mediterranean Flank Steak

Makes 4 servings • Serving size: 6 oz. steak
Prep time: 5–10 min. • Marinating time: 4–8 hours
Cook time: 10–20 minutes

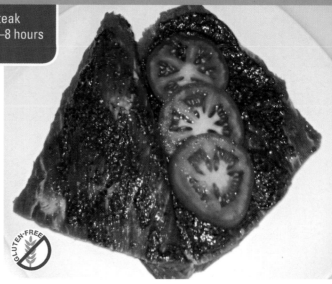

 **What you'll need:**

1.5 pound organic, grass fed flank steak with fat trimmed off

2 Tbsp pesto *(see recipe for Basil Pesto)*

1 organic Roma tomato, sliced

¼ tsp sea salt

**FLANK STEAK** pictured is marinating.

**1** Butterfly the flank steak by cutting in half lengthwise.

**2** Rub the inside of the steak with pesto.

**3** Place tomatoes on pesto. Close the steak. It will look like a sandwich with the tomatoes in the middle.

**4** Sprinkle outside with the salt.

**5** Grill 5–10 minutes each side. Grilling for 5 minutes on each side will result in rare to medium rare. You can increase grill time to your desired temperature.

*\*Contact manufacturer to ensure product is gluten-free.*

---

 **Chef's Serving Suggestions**

- Serve with the *Salad Caprese.*
- Try with *Mediterranean Zucchini* or grilled summer vegetables such as zucchini or asparagus.

Makes 4 servings
Serving size: 1 Hake fillet & 1 cup bok choy mix
Prep time: 5–10 minutes • Cook time: 30–40 minutes

## What you'll need:

1 pound wild caught Hake fish loins *(fillets)*, thawed

⅓ cup *Black Bean and Garlic Spread (see recipe page 101)*

1 head bok choy, chopped

½ cup pre-cooked black beans*

2 Tbsp red onions, minced

10 oz. extra firm tofu,* cut into strips

**1** Pre-heat oven to 350°.

**2** Line a casserole dish with parchment paper.

**3** Layer black bean spread evenly onto the tops of the pieces of hake.

**4** Combine bok choy with black beans and onions.

**5** Spread bok choy mix in bottom of dish.

**6** Layer the tofu strips over the bok choy mix.

**7** Place the hake loins on top.

**8** Bake uncovered for 30–40 minutes.

*Contact manufacturer to ensure product is gluten-free*

## Chef's Serving Suggestions

- Try this with 1 cup diced organic tomatoes or halved organic cherry tomatoes. Mix the tomatoes in with the bok choy and black beans at step # 4.

- Hake can sometimes be difficult to find, but it is worth the effort. It is a flat fish similar to halibut. Halibut can be substituted in this recipe. Halibut fillets tend to be larger than the hake, so you may have to increase cook time.

- Haddock, cod or sole can also be substituted. Cook times will vary if substituting with one of these fish.

# Red Snapper or Yellow Fin Tuna with Thai Sauce

Makes approximately 4 servings
Serving size: 6 oz. fillet
Prep and cook time: 30 minutes

## What you'll need:

1 Tbsp coconut oil

4 red snapper or yellow fin tuna fillets *(4 to 6 oz. each)*

2 cups Thai Sauce *(see recipe on page 135 to prepare)*

3 cups chopped organic spinach or bok choy

1 cup organic cherry tomatoes *(optional)*

GLUTEN-FREE

**YELLOW FIN TUNA** has beautiful, bright red meat

**RED SNAPPER**

1 Heat coconut oil in a 12" sauté pan on medium-high until oil just begins to ripple.

2 Add the fish and sear 1 to 2 minutes on each side, starting with skin side down.

3 If you prefer your fish cooked a bit more, after searing add the fish to the simmering liquid in step 6 of the *Thai Sauce* recipe, until it reaches desired inner temperature. This can take up to 5 minutes for well done yet still tender fish. (Tuna can cook up to 7 minutes.)

 **Chef's Serving Suggestions**

- Place ¾ cup chopped fresh organic baby spinach or chopped fresh bok choy greens in the bottom of a soup bowl.

- Top the greens with one fish fillet.

- Pour ½ cup *Thai Sauce* over fish and top with ¼ cup organic cherry or grape tomatoes.

- This plate is beautiful and delicious. Enjoy a salad or side of steamed veggies to make it a complete meal.

# Thai Sauce for Fish Fillets

Makes approximately 4 servings
Serving size: ½ cup
Prep and cook time: 30 minutes

## What you'll need:

1 Tbsp olive oil

⅓ cup onions, chopped

3 cloves fresh garlic, chopped

1 tsp lemongrass, chopped

3½ cups low sodium chicken or vegetable stock*

1 Tbsp fresh ginger, finely chopped

2 Tbsp sake*

1 tsp raw agave nectar*

½ tsp sesame oil* *(optional)*

¼ tsp Tamari sauce*

5–10 baby bellas *(baby Portobello mushrooms)*

**LEMONGRASS** can be found packaged in most grocery stores, in the refrigerated section with other fresh herbs. Lemongrass is used to flavor broths and soups, but should be strained out before eating. It is very tough and has a tree bark like texture.

*Contact manufacturer to ensure product is gluten-free*

1. In a medium pot over medium-high heat, combine olive oil, onions, garlic, and lemongrass.

2. Sauté for 3 minutes then add stock and ginger.

3. Bring to a slow boil and reduce heat to medium so that sauce is just boiling (not a full rolling boil).

4. In a separate bowl, whisk together sake and agave nectar. Add to simmering sauce.

5. Continue to simmer for 10 minutes.

6. Strain liquid to remove all solids.

7. Return to pot, add mushrooms, sesame oil, Tamari sauce, and simmer for additional 5 minutes.

### Chef's Serving Suggestions

- Serve with red snapper or yellow fin tuna fillets as prepared on page 134.

- To spice it up a little, add 3 or 4 drops of Thai chili oil or ¼ tsp finely diced fresh cayenne pepper.

- For you curry fans, adding ¼ tsp red curry paste would also be excellent.

- You can also use this sauce to poach red snapper, ocean perch, sea scallops, muscles, or yellow fin tuna fillets by adding the raw fish in step #7 and cooking at just boiling for 5–7 minutes (cooking times will vary depending on the type and size of fish being poached).

# Fish Bedding

Makes 2 servings
Serving size: 2 cups
Total prep time: 10 minutes

 **What you'll need:**

1½ cup bean sprouts, chopped

1 cup black beans *(pre-cooked, or drained and rinsed if using canned)*\*

2 cups organic baby spinach, chopped

2 Tbsp organic feta cheese\*

¼ cup raw, unsalted pine nuts or macadamia nuts,\* chopped

2 Tbsp fresh cilantro, chopped

2 tsp olive oil

¼ tsp sea salt

4 organic Roma tomatoes, diced

**RARE TUNA** is shown on *Fish Bedding.*

❶ Mix all ingredients together.

❷ Serve under your favorite grilled fish to make a complete meal.

*\*Contact manufacturer to ensure product is gluten-free.*

 **Chef's Serving Suggestions**

- You can eat this gorgeous green salad alone or use it as the perfect accompaniment to your favorite baked, broiled, or grilled wild caught fish or lean organic meat. It is especially good with rare tuna!

# Savory Pesto Salmon (Jack's Favorite!)

Makes 4–6 serving
Serving size: 5 oz. fillets
Total time: 1 hour

## What you'll need:

2 pounds asparagus, ends trimmed off

¾ cup beans *(any type, pre-cooked or canned\*)*

¼ cup red onions, minced

1 Portobello mushroom cap, coarsely chopped

2 pounds skinless wild caught salmon, cut into 4–6 pieces

1 Tbsp pesto\* *(see Basil Pesto recipe to ensure this is gluten-free)*

1¼ cup low-sodium stock\* *(chicken or vegetable)*

**JACK ZIMMERMAN** is a close friend and supporter of *The Healthy Edge*. This could be a weekly dinner at his house! He gave it two thumbs up and you will too!

① Pre-heat oven to 350°.

② Line bottom of a casserole dish with parchment paper or lightly brush bottom with olive oil.

③ Spread asparagus in bottom of dish.

④ Mix beans and red onions and sprinkle over asparagus.

⑤ Layer the Portobello pieces over the beans.

⑥ Spread the pesto evenly on one side of each piece of salmon.

⑦ Pour stock then place salmon over asparagus.

⑧ Cover with aluminum foil and bake 35–45 minutes.

*\*Contact manufacturer to ensure product is gluten-free.*

# Grilled Red Snapper Fillets

Makes 2 servings
Serving size: 1 fillet
Grill time: 6–8 minutes

 **What you'll need:**

2 wild caught red snapper fillets,
4–5 oz. each

1 tsp fresh thyme, chopped
*(1/2 tsp dried)*

¼ tsp sea salt

1 clove garlic, chopped

1. Rub the fillets with the thyme, salt, and garlic. Allow to marinate for 10 minutes to 24 hours in the fridge.

2. Grill the snapper skin side down first, for 3–4 minutes on each side.

 **Chef's Serving Suggestions**

- When cooking fish, always grill or sear the skin side first.
- Serve this snapper with a generous side of any *Healthy Edge* approved salad or veggie side dishes.

# Broiled Salmon on Fresh Thyme

Makes 4 servings • Serving size: 4 oz. fillet
Total prep and cook time: 10–15 minutes

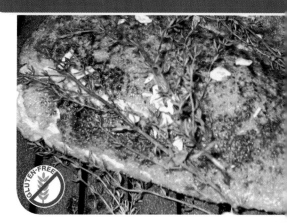

 **What you'll need:**

4 skinless wild caught salmon fillets, 4 oz. each

1 Tbsp coconut oil

8 sprigs fresh thyme

1 tsp olive oil or olive oil cooking spray

1. Preheat oven to 350° and prepare a broiler pan with olive oil or spray or line with parchment paper.

2. In a 10" sauté pan, heat coconut oil over medium-high heat.

3. Place fresh thyme in pan and place salmon atop the fresh thyme sprigs.

4. Sear salmon for 2 minutes on each side, leaving the thyme in the bottom of pan when turning the salmon over.

5. Transfer the salmon to the broiler pan, with the thyme underneath each piece.

6. Bake in oven for 8–10 minutes.

 **Chef's Serving Suggestions**

- This salmon recipe is great served with asparagus. Try it with the *Tomato Caper Sauce* recipe.
- You can also sprinkle the raw salmon with some Ezekiel bread crumbs or 100% whole grain cracker crumbs before searing in step 3. This would not be gluten-free.

# Swordfish Steaks

Makes 3 servings
Serving size: 1 swordfish steak
Marinate: 8 hr. overnight • Cook time: 10–15 min.

 **What you'll need:**

3 wild caught swordfish steaks,
   4–5 oz. each *(fresh or thawed)*

3 Tbsp olive oil

2 tsp or 2 cloves garlic, minced

1 pinch sea salt

½ tsp chopped fresh rosemary *(¼ tsp dried)*

1 tsp chopped fresh thyme  *(½ tsp dried)*

 **Grilling Directions:**

1. Heat grill to 350°.

2. Grill each swordfish steak about 5 minutes on each side. (Cook times may vary depending on grill heat and thickness of swordfish). Make sure to serve fully cooked.

 **Stovetop/Oven Directions:**

1. Preheat oven to 350°.

2. Heat a 12" sauté pan over medium high heat.

3. Pour some of the excess olive oil (from marinade) into pan.

4. Sear swordfish for 2 minutes on each side, until well browned.

5. Place in oven on a broiler pan for 5–8 minutes or until cooked throughout.

## Prep Before Cooking:

1. Place swordfish steaks in a bowl.

2. In a separate bowl, mix all ingredients together. Pour over swordfish steaks.

3. Let marinate overnight or at least 8 hours.

4. Cook on grill or stovetop/oven.

 **Chef's Serving Suggestions**

- This fish goes well with hearty vegetables like carrots or a delicate organic spinach salad. Try with the *Celery Root Puree* recipe.

- This marinade is easy to throw together the night before or in the morning. The fish will be best marinated at least 8 hours. This allows it to soak in the fresh garlic and herb flavors.

# Steamed Cod

Makes 3 servings
Serving size: 1 cod fillet
Total time: 10–15 minutes

## What you'll need:

3 pieces wild caught, center cut cod loin

6 sprigs fresh thyme

3 sprigs fresh rosemary

2 organic Roma tomatoes, cut in half lengthwise

Bamboo Steamer or double boiler pot

**BAMBOO STEAMER**

1. Place 1–2 inches of water into the bottom of a double boiler pot or into a 12" skillet.

2. Heat on high heat until water is at a full rolling boil.

3. Arrange cod in the top tray of a bamboo steamer or in the tray of a double boiler. Layer as follows: 2 sprigs thyme, 1 sprig rosemary, 1 piece cod, and ½ tomato.

4. Place bamboo steamer tray (or double boiler tray) into boiling water.

5. Steam cod on high heat while still at full rolling boil, for 7–12 minutes (depending on thickness of cod).

6. Cod is fully cooked when tender and flaky (when it pulls apart easily).

 **Chef's Serving Suggestions**

- Bamboo steamers are a fantastic addition to any kitchen. They can be purchased in most kitchen supply stores. It is a great way to cook healthy fish and vegetables.

- Add whole heads of baby bok choy, asparagus, or cauliflower into the tray and steam with the cod. Some vegetables, such as carrots, need more time to cook. If you choose to steam carrots with the cod, remove the cod when fully cooked and allow carrots an additional 3–4 minutes in the steamer.

## I'M A SUGAR-HOLIC

**MY NAME IS CINDY AND I'M A RECOVERED SUGAR-HOLIC.** Most people know me as Cindy, the athlete. I love to run, bike, hike, Nordic ski, and snow shoe. I competed as a distance runner in college and to celebrate my 50th birthday in 2007, I ran in a 50-mile ultra marathon. On the outside I was thin and seemingly fit. Most people probably considered me healthy. What they didn't know was that I had a sweet tooth. I was addicted to sugar.

Through my exercise I was able to 'mask' my addiction much like an alcoholic is able to function in the everyday world. But on the inside, my labs told a different story. I had high cholesterol. Another strike against me was my family medical history. My mom died at age 55. She was a diabetic and died of a heart arrhythmia. My dad was also a diabetic. He had a stroke and heart attack in his later years and died suddenly. I brushed these off, saying it couldn't happen to me because I was in such good shape. But, when my sister had two strokes and my younger brother had a major heart attack within a month of each other, I knew I couldn't ignore the facts any longer. Something needed to change.

I was introduced to *The Healthy Edge* and began changing my health from the inside out. I learned that sugar was the culprit in my life and no amount of miles could counteract its affect on my health. The knowledge I gained from *The Healthy Edge* seminars allowed me to find alternatives and make healthy choices. I love the way I eat and feel now. The cravings for sugar are gone. Now I choose my food instead of it choosing me.

In just over four months, my total cholesterol came down 38 points. I improved my marathon time by 18 minutes. But most importantly is the change in my family. My husband weighs less than 200 pounds for the first time in 25 years. His high blood pressure is down in the normal range and he has started running with me. His 'skinny' jeans are too big. My daughter packs a snack to eat in the hall between classes and ran a personal best in her final cross-country season. She looks at food labels with an educated eye and knows what low-glycemic means.

Thank you, *Healthy Edge*. You've helped me become healthy on the inside and overcome a heritage of degenerative disease in my family.

## CINDY WEAVER, USA

**NOTHING WILL WAKE YOU UP LIKE HITTING 40, BUT 41 IS EVEN A BIGGER EYE OPENER!** Starting my family later in life, I have three young children at home who require much of my time and attention. My daily struggle is to keep all of my plates spinning at the same time—work, kids, home, relationship—and attempt to have some sort of life for myself.

I discovered the "F" word (forty) not to be so bad. Well, it certainly wasn't fatal! I discovered a new part of my life beginning—a healthier life. I needed to release about 30 pounds and had a strong desire to see what my body could do (and look like) at 40. I began my new *Healthy Edge* lifestyle and was amazed not only that it *worked* but that it was *easy!*

I have more energy during the day, I have released over 40 pounds, and I am able to easily manage my weight. I developed a passion for running, began training for triathlons, and even started playing hockey with the men! I skate circles around the twenty-somethings and I think I feel better than most of them! I even sleep better, which is a necessity in my life. All of these improvements have led to a major transformation in my mood (with fewer swings to the dark side) which is probably the best perk for my family and friends.

If you are struggling with the demands of your daily life, know that there is something better. Make today the day you begin to take better care of yourself!

Commit to living your best life.

Commit to *The Healthy Edge* lifestyle.

You'll be glad you did!

## MELANIE HANISCO, USA
**RELEASED 40 POUNDS**

# Granola Bars

Makes 10–12 servings
Serving size: 1 granola bar
Prep time: 10 minutes • Bake time: 27 minutes

## What you'll need:

⅓ cup natural peanut butter* *(or other natural nut butter)*

⅓ cup honey

2 Tbsp evaporated cane juice crystals *(pure cane sugar)*

1 tsp pure vanilla extract* *(alcohol free)*

2 cups slow cook thick cut oats*

¾ cup oat bran*

2 Tbsp ground flax seed

½ cup raw, unsalted sliced almonds*

¼ cup roughly chopped raw, unsalted cashews*

⅓ cup organic raisins

1. Preheat oven to 350°. Line an 8"x 10" or 9" x 13" baking dish with parchment paper.

2. In a bowl, combine oats, oat bran, flax seed, and nuts.

3. In a sauce pot, combine together nut butter, honey, cane juice crystals, and vanilla over medium heat. (Watch this closely and do not let it boil.)

4. Once nut butter mixture is melted, use a wooden spoon to stir it into the dry ingredients until well combined.

5. Pour mixture into lined baking dish and use another piece of parchment paper to press it firmly into the dish.

6. Bake 25 minutes.

7. Remove from oven and place dish on a cooling rack. Allow granola bars to cool completely before cutting into 10–12 bars.

*Contact manufacturer to ensure product is gluten-free.*

### Chef's Serving Suggestions

- Substitute other raw, unsalted nuts or seeds for the cashews and almonds. Be creative!

- Avoid adding more ground flax seed. It will make the bars crumble easily instead of holding together.

- If you try to cut these when they are still warm or hot, they will crumble and not hold together. Be patient and allow them to cool completely.

# Basic Granola

Makes: 8 servings • Serving size: ½ cup
Prep time: 10 minutes
Cook time: 20–25 minutes

## What you'll need:

2 cups thick cut slow cooking oats*

½ cup oat bran*

½ cup sliced or chopped raw, unsalted almonds, walnuts, pecans, or cashews*

½ cup mixed raw, unsalted pumpkin seeds, sunflower seeds and coconut flakes*

3 Tbsp ground flax seeds

¼ tsp ground cinnamon*

½ cup honey

½ cup organic raisins or other unsweetened sulfite-free dried fruit* *(optional)*

---

### Chef's Serving Suggestions

- Mix with some organic low-fat plain yogurt, organic Greek style yogurt, or organic cottage cheese with fresh fruit.

- Create a yogurt parfait dessert by layering fruit, yogurt, and granola in a trifle bowl.

- Use as a topping for oatmeal or eat as a cereal.

- Use a variety of raw unsalted nuts and seeds to create different flavors.

- Substitute raw agave nectar for honey.

- Substitute whole millet or buckwheat for the oat bran. This would not be gluten-free.

- Use 2½ cups oats instead of oat bran. Adding the oat bran helps the granola to clump together.

---

❶ Preheat oven to 325°.

❷ Line the bottom of a broiler pan with a piece of parchment paper.

❸ Combine all dry ingredients together in a large bowl, except dried fruit.

❹ Stir honey into dry ingredients.

❺ Mix well and transfer mixture to the paper lined pan.

❻ Bake 20–25 minutes. Using a wooden spoon stir after 7 and 14 minutes.

❼ Remove from oven when granola is a light brown color throughout.

❽ Pick up parchment paper corners and pour granola into a bowl.

❾ Stir in dried fruit. Stir occasionally as granola cools. Store in an air tight container.

*Contact manufacturer to ensure product is gluten-free.*

# Baked Apples

Makes 6 servings • Serving size: 1 apple
Prep time: 5 minutes
Cook time: 2 hours in oven

## What you'll need:

6 organic Fuji apples

¼ cup Zante currants

¼ cup organic golden raisins

¼ cup organic seedless raisins

½ cup whole rolled oats*

½ cup raw, unsalted cashews*

¼ tsp ground cinnamon*

Olive oil or spray or coconut oil

**ZANTE** currants are small, seedless, dried black grapes typically used in cooking, especially baking. Zante currants should not be confused with the fresh sour berries known as currants (black, red, white). Substitute raisins or golden raisins for baking.

❶ Preheat oven to 275° and spray a casserole dish with olive oil cooking spray or lightly coat with olive oil or coconut oil.

❷ In a medium bowl, mix together the Zante currants, raisins, oats, cashews, and cinnamon.

❸ Wash and hollow out the apples (remove core).

❹ Stuff apples with filling.

❺ Bake for 2 hours.

*Contact manufacturer to ensure product is gluten-free.*

 **Chef's Serving Suggestions**

- This is a great dessert that your kids will love!
- You could make the stuffing mixture up to a day ahead of time. Core and stuff the apples just before baking.

# Baked Vanilla Pears

Makes 4 servings • Serving size: 1 pear
Prep time: under 10 minutes
Bake time: 30–35 minutes

 **What you'll need:**

4 organic Seckel pears

¾ cup organic unsweetened apple juice*

¼ tsp pure vanilla extract* *(alcohol free)*

½ cup raw, unsalted walnuts* *(halves are preferred over chopped)*

❶ Preheat oven to 350°. Line a small casserole dish with parchment paper (or lightly coat casserole dish with coconut oil).

❷ Cut pears in half. Scoop out seeds.

❸ Place pear halves open/cut side down in pan.

❹ Toss walnuts in pan.

❺ Whisk together vanilla and apple juice until well combined.

❻ Pour juice and vanilla mixture over pears.

❼ Bake 30–35 minutes uncovered.

❽ Allow pears to cool 5 minutes before serving.

❾ Drizzle juice sauce over pears when serving.

*Contact manufacturer to ensure product is gluten-free.*

**SECKEL PEARS** are small pears with brownish, yellow skins, most often having a dark reddish blush. They are very sweet and juicy with a rather thick and grainy texture.

 **Chef's Serving Suggestions**

- This is great to prepare ahead of time and place in the oven as you sit down for dinner. After dinner the pears are ready to eat.

- Try them topped with a dollop of organic low-fat plain or Greek style yogurt.

- When possible, use 1/2 vanilla bean instead of vanilla extract. Split bean and scrape inside with a knife removing pulp. Whisk vanilla pulp with juice. This will give a smoother vanilla taste.

# Stuffed Baked Pears

Makes 4 servings • Serving size: ½ stuffed pear
Prep time: under 10 minutes
Bake time: 30–35 minutes

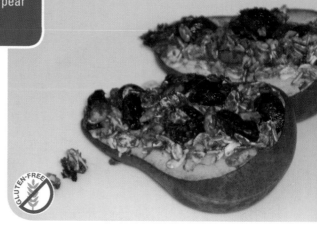

 ## What you'll need:

2 organic Bosc pears

⅓ cup raw, unsalted almonds,* chopped or sliced

3 Tbsp raw, unsalted pine nuts*

¼ cup dried cherries* *(unsweetened)*

2 tsp milled flax seed

¼ cup whole oats*

2 Tbsp raw agave nectar*

① Preheat oven to 350°. Line a broiler pan with parchment paper.

② Cut pears in half. Scoop out seeds and some of the pear flesh to leave a space for stuffing.

③ Mix all other ingredients together.

④ Stuff each pear half with ¼ cup filling.

⑤ Bake 30–35 minutes.

⑥ Allow pears to cool 5 minutes before serving.

*Contact manufacturer to ensure product is gluten-free.*

**BOSC PEARS** (pronounced bahsk) are rather large pears with tender skins. These firm and crunchy pears are favorites for cooking because they hold their shape very well.

 ### Chef's Serving Suggestions

• This is great to prepare ahead of time and place in the oven as you sit down for dinner. After dinner they are ready to enjoy.

# Chunky Lots O' Love Cookies

Makes about 2½ dozen • Serving Size: 1 cookie
Prep time: 30 minutes • Cook time: 8 minutes

### What you'll need:

⅔ cup natural peanut butter

⅔ cup unsalted butter

¼ cup brown sugar

½ cup agave nectar

¼ cup honey

3 cups whole oats

1 cup stone ground 100% whole wheat pastry flour

¼ tsp ground cinnamon

½ tsp baking soda

¼ tsp sea salt

⅓ cup organic low-fat plain yogurt

1 cup organic raisins

1 cup raw, unsalted walnuts coarsely chopped

⅓ cup dark chocolate chips *(optional)*

1. Pre-heat oven to 350°.

2. Mix together peanut butter, butter, brown sugar, agave, and honey until creamy.

3. Stir in oats until well combined.

4. In a separate bowl, combine flour, cinnamon, soda, and salt.

5. Incorporate dry ingredients to mixture alternating with yogurt as needed.

6. Stir in raisins, nuts, and chocolate chips.

7. Drop 1 rounded Tbsp cookie dough onto ungreased cookie sheet.

8. Bake 8 minutes or until light brown.

9. Let cool on cookie sheet for 1–2 minutes then transfer to cooling rack.

 **Chef's Serving Suggestions**

- These cookies are chewy and chunky and have a light, almost cake-like consistency instead of the heavy buttery traditional cookie.

- Kids loved these! What a great treat to bring into school functions!

- Let your kids help you make these yummy treats. They can work on fine motor skills by having them measure and pour from the measuring cup. It is also great practice for older kids to work on their math skills and fractions. It's just plain fun!

- Remember, these are a "healthier" version of traditional cookies, but they are still desserts! Moderation is the key!

# Cantaloupe-Mango Popsicles

Makes 2 cups mix or 4 popsicles
Serving size: 1 popsicle • Prep time: 5 minutes
Freeze for 6–8 hours

### What you'll need:

½ cantaloupe *(peeled and seeds removed)*

½ mango *(peeled and pit removed)*

2 tsp raw agave nectar*

1. Cube cantaloupe and mango.

2. Place all ingredients in blender until liquefied.

3. Pour into a popsicle form and freeze 6–8 hours.

   *Contact manufacturer to ensure product is gluten-free.*

# Banana-Mango Popsicles

Makes 2 popsicles • Serving size: 1 popsicle
Prep time: 3 minutes • Freeze for 6-8 hours

### What you'll need:

½ banana

½ mango, peeled and cut into chunks

3 Tbsp organic low-fat plain yogurt*

1. Combine all ingredients together in blender and pour into popsicle molds or ice cube trays.

2. Freeze 6–8 hours and enjoy.

   *Contact manufacturer to ensure product is gluten-free.*

# Mixed Berry Popsicles

Makes 3 popsicles • Serving size: 1 popsicle
Prep time: 5 minutes • Freeze for 6–8 hours

## Chef's Serving Suggestions

- You can make many variations of this yummy dessert for kids (and adults too).
- Freeze the liquefied fruit in ice cube trays and use in a punch.
- Add 4 or 5 mint leaves to the liquefied fruit and mix with 2 cups cold sparkling water for a refreshing healthy drink.

## What you'll need:

½ banana

6 organic strawberries, stems removed and chopped

2 Tbsp organic blueberries *(about 10–12)*

2 Tbsp all-natural white grape juice

4 Tbsp organic low-fat plain yogurt*

1. Combine all ingredients together in blender and pour into popsicle molds or ice cube trays.

2. Freeze 6–8 hours and enjoy.

*Contact manufacturer to ensure product is gluten-free.*

# DESSERTS

# HEALTHY KIDS

**All parents want their children to live long and healthy lives.** It is so easy to let our lives get busy and often we find ourselves caught in the trap of not making health a number one priority in our homes. Our kids are watching us. Everyday we are teaching them how to eat and exercise and live through the choices we make for ourselves.

With all the demands on families these days, we are providing you with a section full of ideas on how to create a *Healthy Edge* household quickly and easily for your family. By putting some of

**Chef Keith & Jackson**

these principles into action, you will soon be on your way to teaching your children the principles of healthy living. You have an opportunity to instill in them habits they will pass on for generations. We tend to do what we are comfortable with, so why not make eating healthy comfortable for our kids?

## HEALTHY SNACK DRAWER

Have a healthy snack drawer that the kids can reach and make sure it remains a "safe" place for kids to go. **Here are some ideas:**

- Small baggies of trail mix using various raw unsalted nuts, seeds, raisins, coconut, etc.

- Dried fruits *(purchase sulfite-free with no added sugars)*

### HEALTHY EDGE **CRACKERS**

- 100% stone ground or sprouted whole grain crackers *(in moderation)*

- Sticks and Twigs by Mary's Gone Crackers *(Flavors: Chipotle Tomato, Sea Salt, Curry)* marysgonecrackers.com

- Mary's Gone Crackers *(Original Seed Cracker, Black Pepper, Caraway, Herb, or Onion flavored)* see website above

- Ak-Mak 100% stone ground sesame cracker or whole wheat round cracker bread ak-makbakeries.com

- GG Bran Crisp Bread brancrispbread.com

- Kashi Heart to Heart Whole Grain Crackers *(Flavors: Original and Roasted Garlic, TLC Crackers are not suggested)*

- Brown Rice Crackers By San-J *(Tamari, Sesame, and Black Sesame flavored)* san-j.com/product_list.asp?id=5

- Sea Crackers by Two Moms in the Raw *(Garden Herb, Pesto and Tomato Basil flavored)* momsintheraw.com

### HEALTHY EDGE **CEREAL**

- Baggies of tasty high-fiber cereal

- Ezekiel 4:9 Cereal *(Original, Almond, Cinnamon Raisin and Golden Flax)*

- Barbara's Bakery Shredded Wheat

- Kashi Go Lean Crunch Original

- Homemade granola
  —See *Healthy Edge* recipe *(page 145)*

### HEALTHY EDGE **SNACK BARS**

- Homemade granola bars or snack bars
  —See *Healthy Edge* recipe *(page 144)*

- Lara Bars larabars.com

- Go Raw Bars and Granola goraw.com

- Baggies of Non-GMO *(genetically modified)* popcorn
  —We suggest cooking the popcorn with coconut oil in a pan. Add small amount of Celtic sea salt for flavor.

**NOTE:** Some of the above items are gluten free, however you should always check the manufacturer to assure the ingredients haven't changed. Be sure to look for the gluten free symbol every time you purchase any product.

# HEALTHY GENERATIONS

## SPECIAL TREATS FOR KIDS

We know that children love candy and anything sweet! All products listed to the right are for those occasions that call for a treat! These are always in moderation! Create an environment where it is not expected every day, but rather is viewed as what it is, which is a treat! All of the following are gluten and wheat free.

- Instead of fruit roll-ups, try Fruitabu: Organic Smooshed Fruit *(gluten-free)* fruitabu.com

- Instead of hard candy, try Yummy Earth: Organic Candy Drops or Organic Lollipops. This is great for Halloween time! yummyearth.com  amazon.com

- Instead of traditional store-bought Popsicles or Flavor Ice, try our *Healthy Edge recipe for* popsicles *(see page 150-151)* in the dessert section or buy Cool Fruits fruit juice freezers. coolfruits.com

*"The Healthy Edge changed my family's life. I can look at food labels and know what is bad and what is good. The Healthy Edge is real life that even a 13 year old can learn and live. It can change your life too!"*

**Kelsie**—age 13

## SNACK DRAWER **PORTION SUPPORT**

Be sure that if you have a snack drawer, you pre-portion them so the kids know when enough is enough. You can have extra snacks for restocking stored on a higher shelf. Try the *One Baggie Rule* (they can pick one thing at a time). Also make sure that if you are giving your kids a "safe snack drawer" that you are okay with them snacking (even if it is right before dinner). It's a great gift to have your kids know that they can eat when they are hungry! It is empowering for you to create a situation where your kids can choose, but they only have healthy choices available.

*TIMELY SNACKS: As much as possible monitor meals and snacks and offer them every 2–3 hours. This will support you in keeping the kids out of the "danger zone."*

## REFRIGERATOR SNACK DRAWER

Have a healthy snack drawer in your refrigerator as well. Remember, have this low so children can reach it. This gives them a sense of independence and provides variety, but all choices are healthy! What a great way to raise a *Healthy Edge* kid!

- Ants on a log: Celery with organic peanut butter or almond butter and topped with raisins

- Pre-cut veggies like carrots, celery, peppers, cucumbers

- Homemade hummus—If store bought, buy organic and follow reading food label guidelines of *The Healthy Edge* at **GetTheHealthyEdge.com**.

- Grapes, cherries, apples, strawberries, blueberries *(organic and washed)*

- Low-fat cheeses: Buy cheese in blocks, cut into fun shapes and then pre-portion by putting 3–4 shapes in a small baggy. Pre-shredded cheeses have additives that prevent clumping of cheese.

- Yogurt in small containers. Be sure that it contains no added sugar or artificial sweeteners. Greek style yogurt is great and kids can add fruit and high fiber cereal to it for a great snack! *(The Healthy Edge has guidelines about purchasing yogurt! Check out the 7 week lifestyle program at* **GetTheHealthyEdge.com**.*)*

- Edamame: Have small baggies full of edamame in the shell.

- Wraps with organic, grass fed meats or eggs and toppings such as hummus, lettuce, cheese and vegetables

  –Ezekiel 4:9 sprouted wraps from Food for Life *(found in the freezer section)*

  –Alvarado Street Bakery wraps (alvaradostreetbakery.com)

  –Look for wraps that are 100% sprouted grains or 100% whole grains instead of just flour. Example: 100% whole wheat flour vs. wheat flour or enriched flour.

- Organic nut butters are great for dipping fruits!

  –There are many varieties that are available that are organic and no salt added. There are also many stores such as *Whole Foods Market* where you are able to make your own nut butter. wholefoodsmarket.com

  –Gluten-free varieties will be labeled as such.

- Make oatmeal in bulk and have it available to reheat. Add raisins, fruit and milk such as almond or coconut milk. Oatmeal is not gluten-free unless labeled as such.

- Hard boiled organic eggs.

*"The most amazing thing I learned in The Healthy Edge is that fast food is made out of a lot of chemicals and is not "real" food. I choose to avoid fast food places. The Healthy Edge lifestyle has changed my mom greatly. Thank you Healthy Edge!"*

**Florie**—age 13

# HEALTHY GENERATIONS

*"I would personally recommend The Healthy Edge by Amber and April to everyone on the planet! I love it! I learned everything you could ever want to know about healthy eating."*

**Dylan**—age 10

## QUICK KID MEAL IDEAS

- Grill extra chicken breasts, slice them and store in the freezer in small zipper bags. You can pull these out and sauté with a little olive oil or chicken broth for quick wraps, salads, and quesadillas.

- Omelets with their choice of fillings. Provide a variety like green peppers, mushrooms,tomatoes, black beans, chicken, etc.

- Quick homemade soups, created with low-sodium or homemade chicken broth and fresh veggies you have on hand. Add some pre-cooked brown rice, lentils, and some of the frozen pre-grilled chicken. Kids love to drink the broth from the soup with a straw. It makes it fun for them and kids will eat more when food is fun.

- Salads, sandwiches, or wraps and let them pick their own toppings or fillers. Give them 5–6 healthy choices and let them build their own. This is a win-win!

- Slow cooked oatmeal with fresh fruit and/or nut "smiley faces" on top. Drizzle with a little agave nectar if the kids desire more sweetness.

- Use whole grain bread, toast it, and build an egg and cheese sandwich, then let the kids help and use different shaped cookie cutters to make fun shapes.

- All Natural Uncured Buffalo Hot Dogs by The Buffalo Guys  thebuffaloguys.com

- Fun finger foods like:

  –A wrap sliced and served with toothpicks (hors d'oeuvres style)

  –Asparagus to eat with their fingers

  –Mini-shape sandwiches as mentioned above

  –Make your own chicken fingers (baked or grilled)

  –Turkey wraps. Choose nitrate-free sliced turkey lunch meat; wrap the turkey around a slice of cheese.

  –Corn on the cob.

  –Fresh veggies to dip in hummus or other healthy dip.

*"I love the Healthy Edge!  It makes me healthy, strong, and so big!"*

**Arleena**—age: 5

# HEALTHY KIDS

## LUNCH BOX IDEAS

School lunches are a battle for many parents. The nutritional content of most school lunches are full of sodium, fat and sugar. Kids have options such as pizza, donuts, fried chicken, fries, hot pretzels and cookies and no parents around them to support them in making healthy choices. Packing your child's lunch is the most proactive decision you can make for their school day. The time it takes to prepare a *Healthy Edge*-approved lunch will fade in comparison to the health benefits and lessons you share with your child everyday!

*"The best part about The Healthy Edge is that you get to eat every two to three hours and the food is REALLY good!"*

**Daniel**—age 12

Here are some "real life" examples from Chef Keith and his wife, Mindy, when their daughter went off to school for the first time last year!

- Quick homemade soups *(Insulated containers keep the soup nice and hot until lunch time.)*
- Wraps with a variety of fillings
- Hard boiled eggs
- Salads with lots of vegetables *(If your child likes any seeds or nuts, you can add this too.)*
- Applesauce *(There should be no sugar added. Pack a little bit of cinnamon or nutmeg to put on top.)*
- Fresh veggies

- Fresh fruits
  - Whole fruits like grapes and cherries
  - Sliced fresh fruits like oranges, apples, and pears
  - Bananas
- Yogurts *(Pack a small baggy of high fiber cereal or granola to put in the yogurt.)*
- Cheese slices or cubes
- Ants on a log
- Homemade trail mix or granola packages
- Stone ground or 100% whole wheat crackers *(suggestions listed on page 154)* with organic nut butter
- 100% whole grain or sprouted grain pasta with marinara sauce. *(Pack some freshly grated Parmesan cheese as a topping.)*

# HEALTHY GENERATIONS

## LUNCH BOX RULES

Here are some examples of "lunch box" rules to follow:

- Pack a hot lunch at least 2–3 times a week *(especially in the winter)*.

- Have peanut butter and jelly no more than once a week. Use homemade, no sugar added jellies, all natural nut butters and whole grain breads or wraps.

- Pack fresh fruit and vegetable in every lunch.

- Keep options minimal in the lunch box. Pack the "main meal" and two small sides.

- A whole lunch can be fresh fruits, veggies, and cheese.

- Pack water to drink. Occasionally flavor it with cucumbers, lime, or orange slices.

- Add a sweet note in the lunch box reminding them how much you love them! You must love them to care so much about their health!

After Kennedy's first week of school, Keith and Mindy had parents and teachers commenting about how healthy their daughter's lunches were. They wanted to know, "How do you get her to eat that stuff?" and they would tell them that "My daughter eats PB&J sandwiches every day." The teachers made sure to walk by Kennedy to see what she was having every day. Many times Keith and Mindy got asked "Can I have the recipe for that?" What a great testimony to living a healthy lifestyle and how much the parents can influence the kids. By packing Kennedy a healthy lunch every day, she, too, made an impact on the other kids, parents, and teachers. Many of the teachers and parents were so intrigued that they wanted to experience *The Healthy Edge* for themselves.

*"My favorite part of the Healthy Edge is that it inspires and encourages people to eat healthy."*

**Kennedy**—age 7

**THE HEALTHYEDGE**
LIVE THE ABUNDANT LIFE

# INDEX